Quality Is Just the Beginning

Quality Is Just the Beginning

Managing for Total Responsiveness

Steve Levit

McGraw-Hill, Inc.

New York San Francisco Washington, D.C. Auckland Bogotá
Caracas Lisbon London Madrid Mexico City Milan
Montreal New Delhi San Juan Singapore
Sydney Tokyo Toronto

Library of Congress Cataloging-in-Publication Data

Levit, Steve.
　　Quality is just the beginning : managing for total responsiveness
　/ Steve Levit.
　　　　p.　　cm.
　　Includes index.
　　ISBN 0-07-037592-5 (acid-free paper)
　　1. Total quality management—United States.　2. Just-in-time
　systems—United States.　I. Title.
　HD62.15.L48　1994
　658.5'62—dc20　　　　　　　　　　　　　　　　　　　93-40727
　　　　　　　　　　　　　　　　　　　　　　　　　　　　　CIP

1 2 3 4 5 6 7 8 9 0　DOC/DOC　9 9 8 7 6 5 4 3

ISBN 0-07-037592-5

*The sponsoring editor for this book was Jim Bessent, the editing supervisor was
Fred Dahl, and the production supervisor was Donald F. Schmidt. This book
was set in Baskerville by Inkwell Publishing Services.*

 Printed and bound by R. R. Donnelley & Sons Company.

 This book is printed on recycled, acid-free paper containing a
minimum of 50% recycled de-inked fiber.

Contents

Preface

I have been conducting seminars on JIT and other world-class methods since 1984. Every time I held a seminar, someone in the audience asked to see the book. When I said there is none, I was told that I should write one. This experience has been repeated countless times over the years. I finally gave in and wrote the book.

What finally caused me to make the time to write the book is my frustration with the lack of progress on the part of U.S. industry in adopting competitive manufacturing techniques. In part, I was told that this was due to the profusion of books currently available on these techniques. There is certainly no shortage of books explaining how to become "the best" at something or, more appropriately today, "world class," whatever that means.

So, how will one more book help? Currently there is a large universe of TLAs, the acronym for three-letter acronyms: JIT, CIM, TQC, TOC, TQM, MNT, MRP, SPC, TPC, CAD, CAM, CAI, FMS, SQC, ad nauseam. When negotiating this forest of abbreviations, how do you choose the appropriate one? And where do you begin, if at all? This book attempts to cut a path through the forest. Clearly, many of the acronyms describe the same thing but with different names, and all the acronyms are related in principle. What appears to be missing is a unifying principle that provides purpose to what and how we adopt our abbreviation.

From this insight was born the concept of *response-managed organization (RMO)*. The ideas presented in RMO are not especially profound. Indeed, they reflect simple common sense, which we all can aspire to and claim credit for. Audiences have told me otherwise—that these insights *are* profound in that they expand on traditional thought. You can draw your own conclusions. Whether they are profound or simply common sense is not really important. What is important is that you benefit from the book. What I hope you will gain is a realization that virtually anyone can adopt these principles, that they are simple and easy to understand and apply, and that by once again daring to be daring we in the United States can recapture our position as the leading industrial nation on earth.

This book is not intended to provide a recapitulation of statistics demonstrating what others have achieved by adopting modern performance improvement methods, our forest of TLAs. Countless research has been done to statistically document the historical course of American industry and its relationship to worldwide industrial competition. You may review these statistics and reach your own conclusions.

The premise of *this* book is that the accumulated body of statistical data points to the need for U.S. industry to respond and adapt to the changes that have taken place, and that continue to take place, in global competition. This change has, for the most part, not been advantageous to U.S. industry, which seems to be in a catch-up mode. This book is written for readers who are ready to accept the challange of the future and who recognize that, if we are to compete successfully in world markets, then we, as a nation, have to develop and adopt a different strategy from the ones of the past. This book suggests what the focus of this strategy should be, and asks that you at least be willing to explore the potential of this strategy as a basis for competing successfully in international markets. This strategy is based on *response,* on the ability of an industrial entity to respond effectively when called on to do so and, even better, to lead its industry in such a way that it provides the benchmark against which others measure their competitive responses.

This book is intended to present a series of ideas and possibilities designed to challenge prevailing paradigms. In particular, the book addresses the prevailing "quality" paradigms. Modern American industry appears to have adopted "quality" as the path to competitive salvation. I believe that "quality," when pursued as an end in itself, misses the point. *Quality programs, without benefit of additional guiding purpose, run the risk of improving what was, instead of preparing for what should and must be.* This book will provide you with new insight into each idea so that you will be able to relate the principles to your own individual situation.

As a final word, when there was a choice between brevity and pontification, brevity always won. If a separate book is required to understand each principle, then the principle is too complex to be effective. The principles and issues raised in this book are presented directly, succinctly, and clearly enough, I hope, to be relevant to most readers.

Those who wish to offer their comments and feedback may write me at Steve Levit Associates, 13233 Hobnail Drive, St. Louis, MO 63146, or call (314)469-6339.

Acknowledgments

There are many people without whose efforts on my behalf, this book would never have become a reality. I would like to express my deep felt thanks and appreciation to all of them. In particular, I would like to single out several individuals who were of particular help in this project; first and foremost Audrey, my wife. She put up with my absences and frustrations while writing the book. She was the barometer by which I was able to judge the readability of the text. We subjected each chapter to what became known as "the Audrey test." Simply, this test determined whether or not she could read a chapter without falling asleep *and* also understand the contents. One of my fears was that I would be writing an insomniacs delight, a book that guaranteed rapid sleep.

I would also like to express my deep gratitude to my sons, Doug and John, who were a constant source of encouragement, support, and inspiration during the writing of this book.

I would next like to especially thank my editors: Jim Bessent, Fred Dahl, and Danielle Munley. Since this is my first book, I embarked upon the undertaking without fully appreciating the effort required or the contribution possible from the editors. Their efforts transformed my crude drafts into a well crafted, presentable, finished product.

Steve Levit

*Since none of us can predict the future,
the best we can do is prepare ourselves to respond
to whatever the future brings.*
STEVE LEVIT

1

Global Competition

The International Challenge

Today, many companies consider the world as their marketplace. Products and services are established that are universal in application and that can be marketed globally. Currently available chip-based technology has effectively eliminated the distance between customer, provider, manufacturer, and supplier. Companies can buy goods and services from anywhere on the globe, and sell them anywhere on the globe. While there are a few exceptions where it is more difficult to support the full catalog of applications, such as in developing Third World or former Eastern block countries, they are so few as to not mitigate the premise of integrated global competition.

There are many changing facets of global competition. Of particular importance is the emergence of global standards of competition. In this situation, those who are most capable of adopting these emerging standards will prosper; those who cannot will be relegated to the less desirable markets. Gone are the times when an individual nation or bloc of nations can dominate international trade through the application of "proprietary" technology or methods that provide a competitive advantage.

This is not to say that competitive advantage is no longer applicable. Indeed, competitive advantage is more critical today than ever before in our history. Today, those who are not able to lead in establishing the parameters by which we define competitive advantage must at least be able to very quickly adopt new competitive strategies when they arise. Those who cannot respond in this manner will lose and lose big. What is becoming painfully obvious is that in the future companies will get only one chance to earn "prime" business. There will be no second chance for those who do not make the first cut.

In the words of the cartoon character Pogo, "We seem to be faced with an insurmountable opportunity."

In this book we examine the parameters that are now defining international competition. The purpose is to understand the issues, and most importantly, to recognize the unprecedented opportunity that this competition provides for American industry.

Now and into the future, competition is and will be defined in terms of response. The ability of companies to quickly respond to ever-changing demands from the market place will determine who wins and who loses the competition struggle.

Response is the benchmark by which success will be measured. Modern competitive companies will be called on to respond in all aspects of corporate endeavor. This requirement will embrace all types of enterprises, manufacturing and service, supplier and consumer alike.

Response-Managed Organization represents the future for any companies that wish to join an emerging community of excellence among global enterprises. We are talking about nothing less than the survival of individual companies and of our nation as a global competitor.

Throughout this book we will examine how the need to respond is changing the nature of competition. We will explore the impact of response on traditional business functions.

We will examine the goal of a response-managed organization, which is to strive to achieve 100-percent quality and to eliminate nonvalue-adding actions. This is the optimum result of the 5-percent rule (explained in detail elsewhere in the book). Once attained, this is as good as it gets. It defines perfection, at least for a brief moment in time. Perfection cannot ever be achieved or sustained over long periods, but is the goal of perfection attainable? Fortunately, it is not—at least not in an absolute sense, for if we ever attained this goal we would suffer from acute boredom stress.

During our journey through this book we will visit many new and hopefully interesting ideas. Let us begin our journey at its end by first exploring how to get there.

Response-Managed Organization: Some Guidelines

To response-managed organizations, excellence is what was achieved yesterday. Tomorrow they will try to do better. STEVE LEVIT

What is this thing called response-managed organization? RMO is the ultimate competitive strategy. Once an organization adopts RMO principles as the foundation of their competitive strategy, they will have reached a pinnacle of performance that stands above all other competitive strategies.

RMO is an exciting new way of focusing an organization's resources. The organization that successfully converts operations to perform at response-managed levels will find that any and all future methods, improvement opportunities, systems, and other activities will be evaluated in the context of their ability to enhance response. Those that add to the response capabilities will be viable; those that do not will be found to have very little to offer.

The response-managed organization approaches virtually all business activities from a different perspective than that employed by more traditional organizations. As a result of this new perspective, RMO will enjoy significant competitive advantage over those more traditional organizations.

Response-managed organizations ask whether the level of performance they provide to their customers is consistent with the level of performance that ideally they desire from their suppliers. The response-managed organization is aware that the company setting customer expectation as their barometer of success will be vulnerable to a competitive threat from the company seeking to provide a level of service similar to what they ideally desire for themselves.

Response-managed organizations look at what they do as being either a customer-coupled activity or a customer-indirect activity. *Customer-coupled activities* have immediate and direct effect on our ability to respond to customers. *Customer-indirect activities* are the things we do that do not directly affect our ability to respond to customers. During the transition from traditional to response-managed performance measures, we will strive to achieve levels of performance that are primarily customer-coupled.

A response-managed organization is a competitively progressive organization. Such an organization thrives in a state of perpetual change. New methods, technologies, materials, techniques, equipments, and approaches are continually being sought. These will, when developed or discovered outside the organization, be integrated into the organization as appropriate. These will, when possible, be developed within the organization, in which case the organization becomes the initiator of what is considered the leading edge.

The alternative to being a competitively progressive organization is to be a competitively regressive organization. The competitively regressive organization clings to the past. This type of organization spends much of its time and resources in attempts to ensure that what was continues to define what is. They usually hope that tomorrow we will discover yesterday, and all will be right again.

Response becomes the final arbiter by which actions are judged. When confronted with a decision, we should ask whether the result of our decision will either contribute to our ability to respond, eliminate a response inhibitor, or convert a customer-indirect activity into a customer-coupled activity. If the outcome of a decision achieves one or more of these ends we should proceed. If the outcome fails to achieve any of these ends, we should most likely not proceed.

Sustainable success is a result of response. When we become responsive we will be successful. If we focus instead on being profitable, then success may be only temporary. The response organization will be profitable; the merely profitable organization will succumb to challenge from the responsive organization.

2

Starting the Transformation

So How Do We Get Started?

The process for transforming an organization into a response-managed entity involves many attributes: empowerment, participative management, self-directed work teams, total quality, communication, technology, to name a few. It is important that we not get bogged down with concepts. A common mistake, which many organizations make, is to assume that, prior to acting, we must learn all there is to know about the direction or program we wish to adopt. This approach seems to be based on a belief that thorough study prior to action will significantly improve the quality of the action.

This is not a productive approach. No matter how well we prepare for action, we should expect the outcome to be less than perfect. *This is always the case.* To think otherwise leads us down the path of ultimate failure. The implication of perfection is stagnation. If what we are now doing is perfect, do opportunities for improvement exist? Those who once believed in their own perfection eventually had to give way to those who improved on "perfection."

Another aspect of the education-first approach is its failure to recognize that methods, technology, and capabilities are ever changing. One can attempt to assimilate all there is to know about a specific discipline only to find that new information evolved while we were learning what was previously known. Not to worry! We have only to assimilate the new information. Unfortunately, in areas that count, new information is always emerging. The education-first approach leads to paralysis through never-ending analysis.

We *do*, however, have to prepare for our journey. Preparation sets the stage for transformation. What we must do is get started. The first steps on the transformation path will be preparation actions.

Preparation

Paraphrasing from *Alice in Wonderland,* "when you don't know where you are going, any path will get you there." But how will you know you have arrived?

What does this have to do with getting started? We will be embarking on a new and exciting journey. Together we will be traveling down the transformation road, seeking a treasure. What treasure will we expect to find at the end of our journey? If we cannot answer this question before we first set foot on the road, we may travel forever, never knowing if we are nearing or distancing ourselves from the treasure we seek. Is there a true path to take on our journey? Or is the issue more complex, involving many possible "paths," each leading to treasure?

For most enterprises, the journey will involve many paths, each yielding treasure. Each path is also a way station on the transformation road leading to the treasure.

Let us therefore examine how the process begins, and then explore the steps for successfully transforming vision into consensus and finally into reality. First we set the stage. We must prepare for change.

Setting the Stage

How can we bring order into this journey, where do we begin? Our journey starts with a vision. Vision translates dreams into expression. Vision challenges, inspires, seeks interpretation, and, most importantly, requires our response. We respond by forming actions that result in the realization of our vision.

This book presents a vision of the potential locked away within U.S. industry. It is the potential to resume a position as the unchallenged leader of the industrialized world, not primarily as a consumer, but as a fully-contributing member. The United States can be not only a member nation that leads in providing goods and services to other member nations, but also a consumer of the goods and services provided by other member nations. The journey, from vision to reality, occurs through the adoption of response-managed strategies.

Those who share in the vision of U.S. excellence are challenged to accept the task of transforming vision to reality. This implies acceptance of the fact that how we are today is different from how we envision ourselves in the future. We are not content with the present; we wish to improve our future. Ours is not to be a blind journey. We will rely on the principles of response-managed competition to guide us on our way. With this realization, we are ready to embark on the transformation road.

Our journey begins with discontent. The initial stirring of discontent can occur at any level within an organization. Discontent can occur at middle management, as well as at executive levels within an organization. However, we should recognize that when discontent starts at other than an executive level, sooner or later executive approval or sanction will be required to successfully complete our journey on the transformation road. Thus, our first step on the transformation road is prompted by discontent with the present.

Our journey proceeds, guided by vision, toward consensus. Consensus grows as vision is extended and shared by others. Our journey may include traveling down numerous paths, each of which leads us farther along the transformation road. Ultimately, everyone within the organization will be called on to join in the journey. However, initially, we may only seek consensus along individual pathways.

Sharing

A vision without an audience is an empty shell lying on a beach: beautiful to behold but incapable of motion other than to be swept along by the tide. Once swept out of sight, it exists only as a memory of what might have been. Transforming vision into reality requires that it be shared with others. The power of vision grows in proportion to the number of people sharing the vision. Only those people sharing the vision have the ability to transform it into reality. Their cooperation through consensus guides us along the paths of change.

Consensus

Our traditional approach to establishing consensus is to separate activities into "we" and "them" categories and then to proceed according to the group we associate with. In this way, we can agree among ourselves that we know the answers and now only have to convince "them" of the validity of the answers, or that we are okay and the problems lie with "them," or that "they" are the ones preventing us from ... whatever. This approach is convenient, providing justification for how "we" perceive events, a target for our discontent ("them"), and a certain degree of vagueness in formulating opinions.

The "we"-and-"them" approach is not capable of making the journey successful. Our goal—to transform the organization into an integrated response-managed operating unit—requires us to take a different approach. Instead of "we" and "them," we must become "us." When all of "we" and "them" work together in harmony, we become "us."

A successful journey usually starts with a group of "we's" who become discontented with the status quo. They begin to realize, "We can do better." This discontent can occur in any area: accounting, production, materials, QC, and so forth.

Transformation Pioneers

The first "we" may therefore be made up of people within a focused group or department. If this group or department decides to embark on the transformation road, they become our transformation pioneers.

In time, the transformation process must extend throughout the entire organization. In most instances individual, isolated departmental improvement does not provide enough of a competitive advantage to be significant. Reaching the treasure at the end of the journey will ultimately require us to achieve integrated improvement, across all departments and functions, to become an organizational "us." The transformation pioneers must, in time, attract other supporters to their cause.

Sharing the Vision

The challenge before our pioneers is to expand "their" vision into a movement that sweeps away resistance to change throughout the organization. Communication, demonstration, and migration are the building blocks of the transformation road. These building blocks lay a foundation on which our transformation pioneers will build their new organization.

The first building block, *communication,* makes others in the organization aware that change is taking place. Typical responses to this knowledge will range from mild curiosity to certainty that the effort will fail. In all cases, communication leads to some level of awareness and varying levels of curiosity.

As curiosity grows, so does the attention directed to the outcome of the effort. Enter the *demonstration* building block. Nothing breeds success like success. It is vital that the pioneering effort be successful. With success, our pioneers have an opportunity to demonstrate the wisdom of their vision to the curious. (The steps we will be discussing shortly are a recipe for success.) People like to participate in success. Once our pioneers are successful, it becomes easier to demonstrate to others how they too may share in the success.

The process of sharing in success allows the vision, which inspired our pioneers to action, to expand into an umbrella which, in time, will cover the entire organization. Numerous techniques can be employed to communicate and demonstrate success. Examples include:

- Recommending selected reading materials to associates.
- Attending public seminars.
- Creating in-house seminars using outside speakers.

- Inviting other departments to attend the seminars.
- Pursuing discussion opportunities with other departments and individuals.
- Referencing competitors or other companies familiar to your personnel.

The thrust of communication is to educate others in the organization. Our pioneers should be prepared to use any device that will educate and stimulate dialogue.

Remember how our transformation pioneers got started. They became discontented with the status quo. Discontent is a natural result when we are confronted with options that allow us to see and evaluate alternative ways to perform traditional tasks. As discontent grows, we come to recognize the extent to which our actions are the result of our paradigms. Education, dialogue, and demonstration have the affect of encouraging the spread of discontent.

The circle is now complete. Changes resulting from improvement lead to ongoing discontent, which leads to further improvement, and so forth.

As we begin to accept the possibility of change, the dialogue of discontent leads to the development of a vision postulating new possibilities. Acceptance of the vision allows the involved group to begin the transformation process towards the realization of a new reality.

We have arrived at the point where a decision has been made to adopt a response-managed strategy somewhere in the organization. What are the steps to successfully traveling along this path?

Transformation

The nicest thing about not planning is that failure comes as a complete surprise and is not preceded by a period of worry and depression.

Transforming what is into what might be can be an easy task for most organizations. This statement may seem to contradict traditional thinking about the difficulty associated with accepting and adapting to change. In reality, change is not difficult; however, how change is introduced and absorbed can make the process of adoption difficult. Change through fiat invariably encounters resistance. The greater the push for change, the more vigorously resistance grows. Change cannot be dictated.

This does not mean that a decision to change cannot be expressed as a directive affecting personnel throughout an organization. It can be, and frequently is, approached in just this manner. What is missing from this approach is an ability to institutionalize change so that the new method, approach, or whatever comes to define a new organizational "culture."

The directed approach to change reflects an environment in which organizational transformation might be difficult to attain. Sustainable success requires a different approach, one involving both the "operational" and the "cultural" elements of the organization: operational to improve the competitive position of the organization, and cultural to ensure the ability to sustain achievements over time.

If change cannot be achieved by directive, what is the alternative? People are willing and eager to adopt change when they themselves are the authors of that change. This is another way of restating our prior objective to transform the organization from a "we"-and-"them" to an "us" environment. When the "us" environment reaches consensus defining the direction, substance, and manner of change to be affected, transformation becomes an easy task.

How do our transformation pioneers create an "us" environment?

Will this approach require them to involve the entire organization?

Will they gain enough support from other departments and functions to be able to proceed with their transformation plans?

Does all this mean that the entire enterprise is expected to become "us" and to immediately contribute the same effort, or to attain equal levels of involvement?

The answers to these and other related questions will be presented in the paragraphs to follow. For now, suffice it to say, not everyone in the organization will immediately join in the journey. While it is true that, "us" are everyone in the enterprise and eventually all of us will have to be involved with the transformation process, this is not how we will start our journey.

Traveling on the Transition Path

We will adopt a multilevel approach, involving an action plan that addresses the "operational" and the "cultural" elements of the corporation. The supposition is that attaining a successful transition is to a great extent a "head game," in which the perception of success enables the transition process to spread throughout an organization. Initial emphasis will therefore be placed on establishing a demonstratable success. Our initial objective will be to identify a process, or part of a process, to transform. We will successfully implement a demonstration process, which incorporates the operational and cultural changes that our pioneers are striving to achieve.

We will then build on the success of our demonstration process to extend change throughout the organization. Each step in this expansion, transformation process builds on all the preceding steps until our transformation road is complete. That is the subject of the next chapter.

3

Ten Steps on the Transformation Road

The transformation process requires that we successfully identify and reconcile many variables. There are too many possibilities for each to be identified and discussed in this book. Many of the variables are environment-dependent and can differ among similar organizations. As a result, this chapter presents only a general outline of the steps required to successfully transform an organization. Readers may then identify the intent of a step and associate it with their own unique situations. The following steps are based on the premise that consensus has been reached to proceed with a transformation project and that some level of management within the organization is supportive of this project. The first task before the authorizing management group is the determination of where transformation should take place or which process will be transformed.

Step 1. Select a Demonstration Process

We will want to quickly establish a Pilot Process that will demonstrate the benefits inherent in a response-managed approach. In addition, a pilot provides the opportunity to develop the procedures and policies necessary to support the adoption of response-managed competitive methods.

The focus of this project will be on reducing the process cycle time and on improving the quality of process results.

If the Pilot Process is manufacturing-related, we can expect to reduce manufacturing cycle time and to improve product quality. If the Pilot Process is related to service or administrative functions, we can expect to reduce the cycle time for these activities, to improve their ability to interact with their codependent functions, and to improve the quality of the output.

Selection of a demonstration (pilot) process is the most important step in our journey. The degree of success achieved in the pilot process can make or break our ability to proceed beyond this initial area.

The pilot can represent any activity within the organization as long as the selected activity meets several criteria:

1. Will the Pilot Process have the greatest potential to be fully and successfully converted to achieve our desired results, to provide significant benefits, and to be low-risk?

- A successful outcome is the most important criterion. The pilot need not be an area or product that will provide the greatest payback, nor does it have to have the greatest impact on the organization. These objectives and benefits will eventually be realized if the pilot is successful.

- If we can attain benefits in these areas in addition to achieving a successful pilot, great. If not, then success takes precedence.

- If the selected process is typical of traditional practices, the contrast to our "new" process will be dramatic. We do not expect these differences to be subtle in nature. Instead, they should be quite dramatic, representing improvement percentages that are very high numbers.

2. Is the labor force associated with the selected process open to change and accepting of new ideas?

- Success is the objective. The possibility of a successful outcome is greatly enhanced when those who participate in setting up the demonstration pilot operation are receptive to change. One of our objectives is to demonstrate the validity and benefit of the new way to perform old tasks. We can strongly illustrate this point if we manage to enlist one of the "skeptics" as a supporter. Who are the skeptics? They can be found in most organizations. They are those who do not believe anything different will work, those who vigorously resist any kind of change.

- The advantage in gaining the support of a skeptic lies in how this will be perceived by others in the organization. The response we are seeking is something like, "Wow, if So-and-so thinks this is a good idea it must be great!"

3. Is the current labor force highly proficient in performing their present tasks?

- If success is our primary objective, the most productive use of resources occurs when those participating on the Pilot Process team fully understand how the job is done today. This knowledge is vital to the transformation dialogue. In addition, those participating in determining how these same jobs will be done in the demonstration line will also staff the demonstration line.

4. If our Pilot Process is in manufacturing, is the selected product capable of being made using a balanced pull-manufacturing process?

- A balanced pull process (which is important, as explained in Chap. 6, "Reengineering for Response") is the goal when transforming manufacturing operations. We may alter this objective when transforming an administrative or engineering process. In these instances our primary goal will be to reduce nonvalue-adding time actions; achieving pull process balance, while desirable, may not be feasible.

- In a manufacturing environment, we can expect to begin our efforts by transforming some manufacturing operations.

5. Is ample space available to accommodate installation of the transformed manufacturing or other process?

- Balanced pull processes use space differently than their traditional nonresponse-managed counterparts. We must be confident that our transformed process can be accommodated in the space available. In most instances, pull processes require far less overall square footage than their traditional nonpull counterparts.

6. Are there any special situations that could jeopardize the success of this transformation?

- It is reasonable to expect that existing processes may contain steps that do not seem to be adaptable to a pull environment. These types of situations can be obstacles to success in that they can mitigate the level of improvement obtained from the transformation.

- We must be prepared to challenge traditional wisdom, which dictates why it is not possible to change the way we are doing things now. I have encountered at least one such situation in virtually every transformation I have been involved with. In each instance the special situation was one that could not be altered. In each instance we ended up altering what was "unalterable," gaining considerable advantage from the transformation.

- There may be, however, physical boundaries that will limit the transformation process. Not all situations can be quickly, easily, or economically reconciled. In the most extreme cases, we should accept that there will be products and processes that cannot be effectively transformed.

7. Does the selected product represent a family of products, or is it a unitary product?

- The economics of change are improved when the process we are transforming can be applied to a family of products or services. If we have choices in selecting our initial transformation process, we should select one that can be easily expanded to embrace other products or services once the initial effort is successful. This ability to easily expand helps to provide further support to a migration effort.

8. Is outside assistance available to help with the initial transformation effort?

- This is a very important question. Rarely does a company have an internal talent pool experienced in these types of transformations. There is no reason to expect this expertise to exist among in-house personnel.

- Can a successful transformation be accomplished without outside assistance? Possibly. But it rarely occurs in a timely manner and, more often than not, it is not successful.

- This takes us back to our education-first approach. This is often an attempt to enlist the in-house ability to lead and manage a successful transformation effort. By taking this approach we are setting the stage for failure.

- We have addressed the need to demonstrate performance, not just speak about it. Our actions must be consistent with our intentions. When our intention is to become a response-managed organization capable of responding quickly to any demands on the resources of the enterprise, our actions must support this intent.

- If we approach response by analyzing instead of acting, we send a message that intention takes priority over action. We start out on our journey demonstrating that in reality it's business as usual.

- The use of qualified outside assistance can enhance your chance of success in a considerably shorter time than is possible without such assistance. Qualified outside assistance can reduce the risk of error (but never eliminate it entirely) that is potentially associated with a quick start approach, and it can bridge that initial gap in education and understanding.

If we take these criteria into account in selecting our Pilot Process we will realize our objectives: to position ourselves so that the transformation process has the highest probability of reaching a successful conclusion. This will provide significant benefits while exposing us to low risk.

Selecting a Pilot Process will usually require a review of existing operations and interviews with select plant personnel.

Once a pilot line candidate is selected, we can move on to the next step in the planning and implementation process. Several actions are associated with this phase of the program.

Step 2. Select a Steering Committee and Project Team

Following the selection of a Pilot Process, we can identify which management and other personnel should be involved in transforming that process into a response-managed entity. At this point we know the people who are currently performing the activities of the Pilot Process and the corresponding management reporting chain.

These people provide a pool from which we can select the people who will be involved in the Pilot Process. We will select both workers and management personnel; the Steering Committee and Project Team are each cross-functional in makeup. This action is aimed at immediately establishing relationships that will be important both to the success of the pilot as well as to the continuing success of the program as it expands throughout the organization.

Any functional activity affects all other functions within an organization and, in turn, is affected by them. In a manufacturing organization, this interdepartmental interaction is amplified. We cannot ignore this interaction.

Creation of a Steering Committee and Project Team provides a unique opportunity for cross-functional dialogue among operating entities within the organization. Participation on one of these teams is typically a new experience for the personnel involved. In most cases, this is the first opportunity managers and labor have had to meet, as equals, in a cross-functional setting and to discuss issues that affect each participant. If the transition process were to achieve no other end than to initiate this type of interaction and communication, it could be considered a success. Yet, the benefits resulting from a cross-functional approach to organizational issues are numerous and provide lasting advantage to the company.

Involvement—Not Just Commitment— from Senior Management

The most desirable situation is one in which senior management is involved in the undertaking. A less desirable alternative is noninterference by management. When all that can be achieved is management "commitment" to the undertaking, then the risk of failure is greatly increased.

The difference between involvement and commitment can be significant. Involvement implies active participation in the undertaking, from its inception through completion and into the future. Commitment too often occurs when management says, "We are committed to this undertaking, *You* make it happen." When management is not actively involved in the process, the risk is that support for the undertaking will be lost when hard decisions have to be made—and they *will* have to be made. Involved management tends to take a "we are in this together" approach. The message is, "we are behind this. How can we work together to ensure the success of the activity?"

By creating a Steering Committee and a Project Team, you will establish a framework in which all parties who are affected by the transition process can be involved. This approach provides a forum for discussion, reconciliation, and agreement on any and all issues associated with the transition effort, at all levels of the organization. There should be no surprises resulting from pilot activities.

The Steering Committee

The Steering Committee should be staffed by senior management from each functional area impacted by Pilot Process activities. In most situations, this includes representation from all functional areas. This committee provides direction, resources, and conflict resolution support to the Project Team. It also provides management an opportunity to clearly demonstrate their involvement with and full support for the project. The Steering Committee should meet with the Project Manager on a regular basis. In most situations meetings should be held no less frequently than once each month.

The Project Team

A Project Team should be formed with representatives from each functional area affected by the transformation effort. Typically, Project Teams include representatives from:

Production workers.

Production supervision.

Manufacturing management.

Manufacturing/industrial engineering.

Research and development.

Finance/accounting.

A union representative (if appropriate).

Purchasing.

Marketing.

Project team members are responsible for developing a detailed transition plan. They also fulfill the role of ambassador between their functional area and the team. In this capacity, they are expected to share team activities with their peers who are not directly involved in the project, as well as to communicate to the team any observations, suggestions, and opinions provided by their peers.

Not all functions are involved to an equal extent in Project Team deliberations. The Project Team is responsible for developing the pilot transformation plan and for successfully implementing the plan. Project team members meet and participate in team activities on a part-time basis.

A Project Manager should be appointed to direct the efforts of the Project Team. The Project Manager position is usually a full-time responsibility. The Project Manager is responsible for leading the Project Team through project activities and for providing guidance and support to team members to ensure that project delivery schedules are on time.

The interaction between the Project Manager, representing the Project Team, and the Steering Committee allows for a smooth transformation for the Pilot Process. The Project Manager will present project team recommendations to the Steering Committee. Acceptance of these recommendations by the Steering Committee provides authorization to implement the recommendations. In this process, there are no surprises at any levels of the organization. The

Steering Committee may disagree with team recommendations or require clarification of specific issues. The Project Manager is responsible for ensuring that dialogue is maintained between the two project groups to reconcile all outstanding issues.

Typically, the Project Manager will meet with the Steering Committee at least once a month unless project requirements indicate the need for more frequent meetings.

If outside support is used, support personnel should be present at all meetings between the Steering Committee and the Project Manager.

Step 3. Hold the Kickoff Event

At this point we know where our initial efforts will be directed and who will be specifically involved in the Pilot Process. The next action is to begin the transformation process.

How the process is initiated determines how the program will be viewed by personnel within the pilot facility as well as throughout the corporation. The "kickoff" event should be a big deal. You want to proclaim loudly and clearly the intention to adopt new methods that will have a positive effect on everyone in the organization. The purpose of a kickoff event is to inform as many people as possible within the organization that something new and exciting is about to happen. This event is used to establish and mold initial perceptions of personnel towards the Pilot Process.

The kickoff meeting also provides project organizers and supporters an opportunity to introduce the program to the facility and to establish a positive expectation towards the program among facility personnel. In addition, this meeting is used to visibly demonstrate that the Pilot Process is important to the future prosperity of the corporation.

The kickoff meeting is a positive way of achieving the objectives discussed in the section on the preparation stage, namely, to create awareness and curiosity towards project activities within the organization.

Acknowledge It for the
Head Game It Is

Managing change is in many regards a "head" game. How you manage perceptions determines the outcome. If change is to be accomplished, people have to believe that change is possible and that change is beneficial to them. The kickoff meeting presents an opportunity to show that our transition pioneers are indeed harbingers of positive change and that this change is desired by corporate management.

This position can be made most strongly when the Steering Committee participates in the kickoff event. For many organizations, this level of participation by senior management is a unique event. Some kickoff events bring together senior management and labor for the first time in corporate history. The outcome of this alliance is always positive, benefiting all participants.

To further reinforce the perception that something important and new is about to begin, the kickoff meeting should be held off premises and include all employees within the transformation facility. Audience size is important. I have found that an effective upper threshold is 70 to 80 people per kickoff session. When more personnel are involved, several kickoff sessions may have to be planned.

How long should each session be? There is no magic length. In general, the sessions should be long enough to clearly communicate project objectives, as well as to provide an overview of how the transition will affect the organization and why that effect is desirable. The meeting should be as brief as possible in order to generate a sense of excitement and anticipation. If it goes too long, there is risk of losing an audience.

We select the Steering Committee and Project Team prior to the kickoff event. We can use the event to introduce the Project Team and Steering Committee to their peers. Members of the Project Team are introduced as representing the interests of their peers in the program.

A successful kickoff event will leave the participants with a sense of optimism, urgency, and anticipation. It is important to build on these expectations. The next phase of the project should therefore begin immediately following the kickoff event.

Step 4. Initiate Project Team Activities

You will want to begin formal Project Team meetings no later than during the week following the kickoff event.

An important facet of team interaction is where they will meet. Whenever possible, a "war room" should be provided to the Project Team. This becomes their room, where they can place materials, charts, or whatever on the walls and leave them there. It is a common ground where all are equal in ability and interchange. Titles and position are left on the doorstep prior to entering this room. In this room all opinions, views, and contributions are valued and will be evaluated equally. We want to use this room not only to initiate and successfully conclude the project but to further instill the attributes associated with high-performance teams within the Project Team.

To quickly develop the skills of Project Team members and to enable them to function effectively, an effective education program is required. Step 6 provides details covering the types of education and training to provide during the transformation process.

The team should accomplish several activities before they begin to design the Pilot Process: to develop a project charter and to document how the target process operates today.

Developing a Project Charter

The Project Team should develop a project charter. The charter identifies the purpose of the project, the results and benefits expected from the project, the people and resources required to accomplish the project, the approach to be taken to successfully complete the project, and the reporting and communication requirements of the project.

The charter is important in ensuring a common understanding of the why, who, and how of the project pertaining to all affected levels of the organization. The act of developing a charter helps team members to clearly and fully focus on the project objectives, as well as their impact on the daily operations of the organization.

The project charter will be presented to the Steering Committee for discussion and approval. The Project Team will proceed with project activities once the charter is approved. In the event that the charter is not approved, it will be returned to the Project Team for further review and resubmittal to the Steering Committee. Once approved, the charter is signed by each Steering Committee and Project Team member.

Documenting the Existing Process

To successfully determine how to transform the existing Pilot Process into a response-managed process, it is necessary to understand how the process works. This understanding comes from documenting the existing process. The present process is analyzed and documented to:

- Provide the actual number of steps.
- Identify each step as (1) process, (2) transfer activity, (3) storage, (4) set-up, or (5) inspection.
- Indicate the status of material at each step: (1) annealing, (2) drawing, (3) washing, (4) storage, (5) transfer, (6) assembly, and so forth.
- Provide comments per step when called for. For example, *transit distance 20 ft.,* or *waste in material handling.*
- Document how many people are involved in performing each step.
- Document how much time each step requires.

Once the project charter is established and approved, and after the pilot process is documented, the Project Team can begin to develop the conversion plan for the Pilot Process.

Step 5. Develop the Pilot Process Conversion Plan

Conversion Plan

The Project Team will use the process documentation to develop a conversion plan for the Pilot Process. When appropriate, a traditional "Work Breakdown Study" format can be used. In this format, a plan is comprised of a "Goal," "Milestones," "Objectives," and "Tasks." Responsibilities are assigned at the task level. The conversion plan should be comprehensive in scope and explicit in detail. The plan provides for the integration of project requirements with ongoing day-to-day activities. The conversion plan documents exactly how the conversion process will take place. A large portion of this effort is directed at developing the new procedures and policies required to support pilot operations.

The plan may even call for the creation of additional teams, which will be responsible for developing detailed sections of the plan.

The conversion plan should be developed quickly. It is important to establish a sense of urgency toward design and implementation of the Pilot Process.

Once this process has begun, it is important to progress at a rapid, steady pace. The people participating in the project should be prepared to commit adequate time to the project to perform at this level. During the first several weeks of the Pilot Process—the first four to five weeks—the Project Team should expect to meet twice each week. Meetings will typically be four to six hours in duration. Following this quick start, the team should expect to meet with the Project Team twice each week. Thereafter, expect to meet at least one full day each week.

Step 6. Develop an Education Program

One of the first milestones to be developed by the Project Team will be education. A typical conversion plan will include planning a multilevel education program.

The importance of education and training cannot be overstressed. Knowledge and, more importantly, the ability to apply that knowledge are the cornerstones of success in any endeavor. Too often, when deciding how to allocate precious resources and revenues, we overlook or understate the value of education and training. These are soft issues from which we cannot always derive hard benefits that are easily identified and applied to the bottom line. This is not the place to expand on the folly of this approach. Instead, let me provide the following observation: "As you consider the cost of education, you must be equally diligent in evaluating the cost of ignorance."

The extent of the education requirement will be determined by the awareness level for group members at the time the decision is made to get started. Books and seminars are excellent ways to acquire education.

A major consideration is who should provide education support. Should it be an individual or a group of people? Should we rely on internal resources, external resources, or some combination of the two?

Those attempting to use a self-education approach should be prepared to attend outside lectures and seminars, seek out reading materials, and visit companies that have been successful in similar projects. Self-education is a long, difficult process with an uncertain outcome.

In most situations, there is no reason to expect the experience to exist within a company. This experience can be gained only through engaging in similar undertakings at other corporations.

For most of us the use of outside assistance is the only practical way to provide start-up education until internal expertise can be developed. There are additional benefits to seeking outside assistance. An outsider should not be encumbered by internal politics or limited by inbred procedures. A good outside resource—and there are very few of these—will be in a position to question internal activities in a manner not usually possible to employees. In addition, a good resource will bring specialized experience in this type of endeavor to the undertaking.

One word of caution regarding how we choose outside help: As a general rule, industry will seek help from those familiar with their industry. This approach may not be beneficial. The problem with industry specialists is that they often have a world view limited to that industry. They will propagate all the inefficiency resulting from a "this is how we do it in our industry" attitude. They are less apt to challenge existing procedures and methods. They do not bring the insight that comes from taking creative approaches to solving problems in radically different industries. Much can be learned, both within and outside "our" industry. We should use *any* resource that can make us successful, regardless of its origin.

It is also important to seek a resource capable of understanding response-managed issues across the widest possible spectrum of corporate endeavor. All too often, expertise is confined within narrowly focused functional areas. Departments become "silos," in which expertise, communication, and function are retained in vertical alignment by tall walls. This type of vertical focus is not conducive to achieving response-managed performance, which is horizontal in approach.

I recommend three specific educational efforts:

1. Basic introductory education for division management personnel
2. Large audience generic education for Pilot Process facility personnel
3. Topic-specific education for the Steering Committee and Project Team members

Introductory Education

This type of program is designed to generally inform division management personnel of the direction chosen to achieve desired objectives. Directed as it is at management, this education provides an introduction to the general elements of the program, why the program was initiated, and the benefits expected from the program. Most importantly, it sets the perception of how and when the program will impact those in the audience.

Large Audience Generic Education

Generic education "sets the stage" for issue-specific education, and establishes a sense of anticipation among all personnel within the Pilot Process facility toward eventually being included in the "new" program. It prepares the facility for the coming changes. This type of program can be presented during the kickoff event. In very large organizations, it may be desirable to establish an ongoing general education program to extend beyond the kickoff meeting. Everyone should be included in these sessions.

One objective, from the onset, is to demonstrate, through actions, a new team spirit. Expect all to be involved participants in this experience. A response-managed organization seeks the involvement of each and every person associated with the organization, no matter what the capacity or function, to actively work towards ensuring the success of the organization. A successful response-managed organization recognizes that:

- All personnel are worthy of equal respect and consideration.

- All are important.

- All have the potential to contribute in a positive way to the lasting success of the organization.

- Good ideas can be found everywhere, not just in the "upper" echelons of an organization.

We want to energize the organization in order to tap into that vast reservoir of capability stored up in each employee.

Issue-Specific Education

This vehicle enables the Project Team to develop a successful conversion strategy for the Pilot Process. It is best accomplished in an informal manner wherein the participants sit around a table and discuss the specific response-managed organization objectives to be accomplished and how they can be applied within the target facility.

This training also develops the skills required to participate in this type of program. It is not reasonable to expect team members to innately possess the skills necessary to perform the requirements of a Project Team member.

Issue-specific education is especially suitable to cross-functional groups, such as the Project Team which must ensure that decisions made to improve one area will not inadvertently have a negative effect on another area. A cross-functional constituency enhances issue-specific education by stimulating dialogue among participants representing different interpretations of common information. Issue-specific education activities continue throughout the life of the project. The Project Manager or a designated trainer should expect to present new topics for discussion at virtually every Project Team meeting.

Decisions on the Education Program

Several decisions have to be made and logistic issues reconciled when establishing an education schedule.

Where Will the Training Be Provided? Choosing a location for training, which should reinforce its objectives, is important. Is there a training facility on premises? Should the kickoff event be held off premises and all other training conducted on site? The kickoff should be an event perceived as having special significance to the organization. The new path should not be viewed as just another program in a long list of similar programs that have come and gone through our past. The desired environment for ongoing Project Team meetings and the issue-specific education portion of those meetings will serve to reinforce a sense of real positive change in all our education efforts.

You do not want to establish or allow the perception that "this too shall pass" if only we are patient. Response-managed organization is too important an opportunity to let pass. It represents the future for companies that wish to join an emerging community of excellence among global enterprises. It involves nothing less than the survival of many individual companies and of the United States as a global competitor.

Who Will Be Trained? You have to determine who is to receive what training. As a general rule, strive to provide a training segment for each person associated with the facility in which the Pilot Process is located.

The introductory training intended for management should extend to include personnel representing all organization functions: manufacturing, materials, accounting, sales, marketing, purchasing, engineering, administration and so forth. Steering Committee members should receive this training, with Steering Committee meetings providing further training opportunities.

When Will the Training Be Provided? A training schedule should be established. The reasons should be apparent: to allow participants to schedule their calendars, to coordinate training activities with the ongoing day-to-day functions of the organization, to establish clear expectations, to schedule the training location, and so forth.

Some training efforts will be one-time events. Others may continue over extended periods of time. To receive maximum benefit from training, course materials should be organized so as to allow students the opportunity to experience topics discussed during training. When long-term training is involved, the training program, once started, should continue at a steady pace. Starts and stops to training efforts tend to diminish their positive impact on an organization and may not result in an advantageous use of resources.

Who Will Do the Training? The existence of various levels of training may require the use of several trainers. The curriculum will also determine how many trainers are needed and what skill levels they should possess. In general, educators should understand the topic areas involved and how to apply the principles espoused. The importance of application cannot be overstressed.

The use of in-house seminars is an excellent way to begin the education process. This type of seminar allows the presenter to become familiar with the specific needs of a company and to customize the presentation to those needs. In addition, the in-house seminar allows a greater audience to economically participate in the education process. It is usually prohibitively expensive to provide a similar level of education to as many personnel by attending public seminars.

If outside educators are used, it is more important for them to understand the principles of response-managed competitiveness (RMC) and its application in general terms than to be expert in your industry.

If there is an internal training department, you may be able to enlist their participation in providing qualified trainers. Internal trainers can be developed by using a train-the-trainer approach, in which designated personnel receive specific training in selected topics with the intention of then assuming internal education and training responsibilities.

If outside resources are not used to support the project, then the Project Team manager should assume the role of trainer.

What Is the Curriculum?   What is the content of the different training programs? To a large extent this depends on the overall level of awareness within the organization, which varies from one organization to the next, as well as among departments within the organization. There are numerous topics to choose from in designing your curriculum: response-managed organization, total quality, just-in-time, employee empowerment, high-performance teams, world-class management techniques, activity-based accounting, specific technologies and their application (such as EDI), participative management, and effective communication, to name a few.

Your curriculum will depend on your specific education needs. One subject I always include in any transformation effort is a discussion of paradigms.

Rarely understood is the impact of paradigms on the day-to-day decision process and on how we each view our participation in the corporate experience. A discussion of paradigms is a good way to begin an education process, since it is nonthreatening and fun to discuss, and it provides an opportunity to examine traditional values from a new perspective. Joel Barker, a futurist, has created an excellent videotape on this subject.

How Shall the Training Be Structured and Provided?   Too often we neglect the how of training and develop courses designed to transfer information, not to increase skills. This is an important distinction. The transfer of information can be academically interesting but virtually useless until the information is put to practical use. The practical use of information results from associating information with application to increase utilization skills. In this regard, understanding the why of things contributes to understanding how to utilize information and improve skills.

I recognized this principle at work when I was learning to downhill ski. A variety of instructors were all eager to demonstrate how to ski and were all patient in encouraging me to do as they did. Under this type of tutelage, I enjoyed steady progress as a skier—steady but not dramatic. Improvement in technique and ability proceeded at a very slow pace. One day, I encountered a different type of instructor. This person did not immediately take me out to the slopes to begin skiing. Instead, we sat down and discussed how skis work. For the first time I learned how the design of a ski contributed to its functioning. I learned *why* skis ski. I learned how and why a ski, naturally, carves an arc in snow, how the ski turns. Armed with this knowledge, we proceeded to the slopes. I was amazed at my progress. For the first time, I did not fight the skis. Instead, I used them and let them do the work for me.

Progress was rapid, and my enjoyment of the sport increased even more rapidly. Eventually, I became a ski instructor. I never forgot the why lesson, always beginning my relationship with a new student with that lesson. This experience has remained with me and affected, in a positive way, how I approach other teaching situations.

Thus, we are faced with the challenge of designing information presentation formats that not only transfer the desired information but also provide opportunity to apply the newly acquired information to daily activities. Developing this type of training program requires an ability to involve students in the education transfer experience. Students should therefore be stimulated by a combination of sources: Material can be presented, discussed, and finally applied in ways that can be associated with day-to-day business applications. Structured this way, the learning experience becomes fun. People can and should enjoy learning and increasing their skills (capabilities). To paraphrase the Chinese proverb:

What I read, I forget.

What I hear, I remember.

What I do, I understand.

It is much more difficult to develop this type of training approach than to pursue the more typical information transfer approach. This approach calls for greater thought applied to how information is organized and presented. Those developing this type of training program need to draw on creative resources beyond just identifying course content.

How Do We Know the Training Is Effective? This aspect of training is often overlooked. No matter how well we structure and present training and education we can always improve on current methods and content. How can we calibrate our efforts to improve areas that need improvement and to maintain areas that are succeeding? How do we ensure that we provide maximum benefit to all students, recognizing that different people learn best in different ways?

Acquiring this information is desirable to ensure that we consistently meet our training objectives. The questions to avoid are, "What's the matter with these people? Why aren't they doing what they have been trained to do?" Usually the answers lie in that they do not know how to apply the information provided in the training.

In most instances, once the idea of improving skills through continued education and training is absorbed as part of the new corporate culture, we will be continually developing new training programs. We must therefore be ever vigilant to ensure the quality of these programs. *The quality of education and training is measured by the extent to which imparted knowledge is applied.*

What Is Our Long-Term Training Strategy? Have we developed a long-term strategy? Should we develop a long-term strategy? The answer to both questions, for a response-managed organization, is yes!

We are increasingly confronted with new developments in methods, technologies, capabilities, applications, and demands generated by the market place. If an organization wishes to keep up with these changes, they have to be able to quickly absorb new information and adapt to the requirements presented by that information. This implies the need for an ongoing training strategy. The moment we stop learning, we become vulnerable to those who have continued to learn and adapt.

The response-managed organization is aware of this situation and will strive not only to remain abreast of new developments but to be recognized as the initiator of new developments. Response-managed organizations endeavor to set a pace that others are forced to follow.

Logistics Issues

We can expect to encounter numerous logistics-related issues, such as travel arrangements to and from training sessions, lodging and/or meal requirements, printing needs, classroom support tools (blackboards or various types, pads, pencils, notebooks, handouts, training aids, and so forth), content sources, reading materials, and so on.

In addition, coordinating training for large numbers of people typically have special requirements. Experience indicates that for events like the kickoff meeting, the audience should contain no more than 75 people. Specific topic education, on the other hand, can involve multiple smaller groups; typically, these groups should be as small as is practical. These requirements can impose the need to schedule a series of training sessions when it is necessary to involve a large population.

Step 7. Develop a Program to Impart Improved Leadership, Communication, and Decision-Making Skills

Education is a track that extends to infinity. Once the education engine leaves the depot, there are no stops along the way; it cannot stop because new cars continue to be added to its load. Knowledge only expands; it never contracts. In our emerging competitive world those who stop acquiring knowledge will find themselves passed by those whose engines continue to run.

The need to increase skills and knowledge affects all departments and activities within a modern corporation. In particular, transformation to a response-managed organization has a significant impact on traditional management methods and approaches. In most instances, the impact is potentially negative. It is vital that our transformation pioneers recognize this situation and adopt measures to ameliorate its effects.

The transformation process is usually more easily accepted by labor than by management. Labor is generally willing to change, asking management only for consistency and support while changing. Management, on the other hand, often feels threatened by response-managed concepts, especially those associated with teamwork and empowerment. The role of management changes from one of intervention in the decision-making process to acting as a supporter of the process. As a supporter, management transfer the decision responsibility to the team. The manager acts to ensure that the team has the resources to reach a quality decision quickly. Management still retains the prerogative of accepting or rejecting the team decision, but, team decisions should rarely be rejected. If management cannot trust in the collective wisdom of the team, when it is armed with required information to reach a quality decision, then one would have to question why the team was formed in the first place.

Many managers also feel that empowerment, the shift of responsibility downward in an organization, is a threat to their traditional authority. They feel as if they are giving up responsibility. If that is the case, they reason, won't the next step be to eliminate their positions entirely?

The transformation process to achieving response-managed organization performance is built on a foundation of trust among employees, as well as a sense of teamwork and cooperation among all organizational departments. Responsive organizations rely on teams and teamwork as an approach to quickly accomplish tasks.

Improving teamwork skills therefore becomes increasingly important as corporations adopt the "team" concept to problem solving. The teamwork environment is enabled and nurtured when management and labor each improve on leadership, communication, and decision-making skills. In combination, these skills contribute to an ability to attain new levels of achievement.

Step 8. Develop the Implementation Strategy Beyond the Pilot Area

The proposed approach to implementing a response-managed organization strategy presumes success. If the preceding seven steps are followed, the transformation process will be a success. Once we start the transformation ball rolling, we want it to continue and to gather momentum until the entire organization has been transformed.

When the Pilot Process has been converted, our initial success can be migrated to the next target process, repeating the steps used for the Pilot Process. In addition, we can begin to consider the application of response-managed principles beyond the pilot area into all departments within the organization.

Planning for this expansion can and should begin while the Pilot Process is under way. There is no reason to delay planning for the future until the pilot is complete. (In fact, planning for future actions prior to the successful attainment of current actions is typical of response-managed principles.) The question is, how confident are we that the current action will be successful? A successful response-managed organization approaches decisions with an expectation of success, which is based on the sure knowledge that all the resources within the organization have been arranged specifically to achieve that result. The measurement continuum shifts from judgements of success or failure to a presumption of success in which failure occurs so infrequently that we can eliminate it from our consideration. Instead, measures that determine degrees of success can and will vary.

The response-managed organization does not delay action pending the outcome of an event for which the probability of success is very high. The organization no longer performs at levels dictated by the rare negative exception or on the basis of the proverbial "worst case scenario."

The Steering Committee, because it includes management representing all departments within the organization, provides a forum in which to develop the Migration Plan. The committee can either elect to develop the long-range plan themselves, or they can designate a team to accomplish this purpose.

The Migration Plan follows the same steps laid out for the pilot: to select the next transformation target, to identify a Project Team responsible for transforming the target, to train the team, to have the team develop a transformation plan, and finally to implement the plan.

This process is continued until the transformation process is complete. In practical terms, once the pilot has been transformed, the migration effort moves quickly. Each new target area within a department requires ever decreasing time to effect a transformation. Each new transformation benefits from the experiences of all prior efforts.

There is an added advantage to identifying a potential next target at the beginning of the transformation process: A member of the target Project Team can be included in the Pilot Project Team. This approach allows us to approach the target process with built-in experience. The target process individual can also act as an emissary to peers, keeping them informed of emerging issues.

Step 9. Successfully Implement the Migration Plan

The Migration Plan is your plan for extending RMC principles within the organization. Now it has to be implemented. Specific implementation requirements for the migration plan may vary according to the individual needs of the area being transformed. The multistep process just described for developing a transformation plan allows for full disclosure and discussion of all factors associated with both the Pilot Process and the Migration Plan. Once agreement is reached on the elements of the plan, the plan should be implemented as rapidly as possible.

It is reasonable to expect that the Migration Plan implementation schedule will be consistent with the urgency felt to adopt this strategy. You should expect this plan to be as aggressive as staffing constraints will allow.

Step 10. Celebrating Success

While recognition of hard work and success is important, an environment of all work and no play can diminish the enthusiasm that people bring to their efforts. A feeling of achievement and success is important to the well-being of those performing the work.

Teamwork

We have been striving to establish an environment in which the boundaries between departments and personnel within departments have been removed. To this end, we have established a cross-functional Steering Committee and Project Team. By working closely together, they will have been able to make a significant contribution to the well-being of the organization. Through these actions, we have begun to instill the spirit of teamwork among management groups, among labor functions, and between management and labor.

By sharing in the celebration of success we further cement these new vital relationships. Sharing in difficult undertakings that reach successful conclusions creates bonds among participants that have no equal. Sharing in current success builds a foundation for continuing future success.

This is exactly where we should want to be.

The approach outlined for getting there is easier to accomplish than it is to describe and explain. The recommendations in this chapter provide for a "quick start" to demonstrate rapid success and to provide the planning foundation for the rapid migration of the program elsewhere throughout the corporation.

4

Building Bridges to the Future: Developing Procedures

A major risk to successful operations is the absence or incompleteness of operating policies and procedures. These provide the foundation to manage the present and, when properly structured, provide a bridge to the future. Yet, in many organizations, operating procedures are not well documented. This does not mean that they do not exist. New employees are invariably provided with copious information describing the company's product or service, its business standards, and its mission. Invariably what is missing is "how the company functions." How we function is very different from who we are or what we do.

In today's highly competitive business environment, world-class performance is a necessity. Implicit in world-class performance is the notion of continuous improvement, an ongoing striving towards ever improving quality and performance standards. A continuous-improvement environment is in constant change. Without the discipline and understanding provided by well documented policies and procedures, which reflect how we function, change often turns into chaos and turmoil.

Trapped in the Present

Very often we find ourselves trapped in the present, especially when the knowledge base of employees becomes limited to understanding only how they perform their day-to-day job tasks. This condition seems to be the norm for most working people. What we do in the present is a reflection of our past. While people may continue to have good ideas, the past invariably imposes limits on future progress. Possibilities beyond the present do not exist because there is no way for them to arise. In the typical situation, people are confined to knowledge of their work group and are rarely aware of how they impact other work groups. They may be aware of how they are affected by the work done by another employee or department, but even this is limited to its immediate impact on their specific jobs. The organization is defined as a collection of individual departments, each performing specific tasks and each apart from the others. Typically, we are so involved in reacting to daily events that there is no time to discover future possibilities. The knowledge base does not extend outward toward what others are doing, but is confined to what is necessary to cope with today. In this environment people may understand what they do but not *why* they do it, except in the most general terms: "This is the way we've always done it," or "So-and-so wants to see it this way."

The path to understanding why we do what we do can be difficult to travel without a guide. Many twists and turns tempt the unwary into reaching easy conclusions but miss the desired destination.

Most organizations must face these difficulties when attempting to develop policies and procedures. It is difficult to progress beyond the present without the support of new knowledge, which expands the internal horizons of possibility. For most organizations this requires the use of outside assistance.

Having confronted this dilemma on more than one occasion, I have created a method for developing procedures designed to assist others in building a bridge to their future. My policy and procedure development process is built around the principle that success involves two distinct activities: preparation and action. Proper preparation sets the foundation for successful action. One without the other rarely leads to success. Preparation without action is an academic exercise having little or no effect on the organization. Action without preparation may not be linked to reality. It can paralyze an organization and lead to disaster. Each is necessary to ensure the success of the other: both are necessary to ensure the success of the enterprise.

Preparation

Proper preparation includes:

- *Management review team*

    COMPOSITION: Management personnel representing each functional group affected by the policy and procedure development effort. In light of the codependent nature of functions within an organization, all function heads should be included in this body.

    RESPONSIBILITY: Review and approve all policies and procedures developed by the procedure teams.

- *Procedure development teams*

    COMPOSITION: Representatives from each functional area involved with a specific procedure or policy under development.

    RESPONSIBILITIES: Development of each specific procedure and related policies. These teams may not include representation from each function in each situation. Instead, the management review team provides a cross-functional review of all policies and procedures.

    This approach ensures complete understanding of the issues addressed by policies and procedures at all levels within the organization. In addition, it provides for a feeling of ownership towards policies and procedures at all levels of the organization.

- *Project charter.* One of the first activities for the development teams is to establish a charter that defines the goal to be realized from this effort, what is being done, who is responsible for the doing, the expected benefits from the endeavor, how this will be done, and the relationship between the development teams and the review teams. This document is presented to the review team for approval. The final copy is formally agreed to by all parties involved and signed to indicate acceptance. This document ensures that all parties engaged in developing new policies and procedures are in full agreement regarding all aspects of the undertaking.

- *Inventing the future.* New ideas and concepts have to be introduced into the organization. This is accomplished by means of mixed media such as video tapes, team exercises, discussion groups, selected readings (brief articles, no tomes), visits to other organizations, attending seminars, and outside assistance.

- *Discovering the present.* (Lay a foundation for what follows.) To develop meaningful new policies and procedures or to revise existing ones, we must clearly understand where we are now and how we function today. With this knowledge and the experience gained by inventing the future, we can begin to determine what we want to do and how we want to function in the future. To discover the present, we have to clearly document the existing process for which we are developing new procedure and policy.

- *Build the bridge.* We are now prepared to develop our new policies and procedures—policies and procedures that will allow us to operate at optimum levels of effectiveness and provide a bridge to the future.

Our bridge is supported by four legs:

1. *What.* Which procedures and policies are needed?

2. *Why.* An explanation heads up each procedure and describes the purpose of the procedure.

3. *How.* Specifically how will we use the new tools and/or methods to perform the designated functions?

4. *How.* Specifically how will we function operationally once we are using the new tools or methods to support daily activities?

This approach establishes an operating environment that is disciplined and flexible. Organizations following this approach are positioned to respond quickly and effectively to any demands placed on them, and lead their competition in the present and the future.

Many readers will recognize similarity between this approach and the steps outlined in the section "So How Do We Get Started?" These similarities are intentional. While my experience is that this approach almost always works—"almost always" because nothing is perfect—I recognize that this approach may not work best for a few organizations. The procedures and policies developed as part of the transformation process are consistent with this approach. Differences arise with the individuals who perform these tasks as part of a larger undertaking instead of as a discrete activity.

❏ ❏ ❏

Providing a Foundation:
The 5-Percent Rule

For most companies, improving productivity and quality can be free. Why then do so few take advantage of these "free" benefits. The answer is simple: These benefits are free only if you know where to look for them. Most companies do not know where to look or what to look for.

The 5-percent rule shows us where to look for these hidden benefits and tells us what to look for. Where this rule came from I do not know, but I have been using it with clients and in public seminars since 1985. It has been presented to hundreds of people, who have made up the audiences of my seminars, and put into practice in numerous businesses for whom I had provided professional services without serious challenge. In only a few instances, someone would quibble that in "their" situation the 5 percent was more likely 8 or 9 percent.

Why is all this background important? Once explained, the rule is so simple that it is treated with disbelief. I have therefore found it easier to build credibility for the rule before defining it. It *is* real! It *is* as simple to understand as it sounds. And it *can* be applied to virtually 100 percent of all business endeavors. When *properly* applied, it *always* yields significant positive results.

What is the 5-percent rule? The rule states that, of the total time invested in each step of a process and accumulated across all the steps within a process, only 5 percent contributes directly to the desired outcome. The remaining 95 percent of the time does not add value to the outcome. To paraphrase Tom Peters, who recently dramatically described this phenomenon, in the average 40-hour workweek, we manage to put in a solid 120 minutes of value-added work, based on the rule percentages. To apply the rule, we therefore have to stop thinking of ourselves as indispensable and start thinking about *what* we do and *why* we do it.

The rule recognizes the fact that *everything* we do is a *process,* that is, an activity involving a series of steps leading to a desired result. Further, it asssumes that, in any process, the time invested in the outcome can be identified and associated discretely with each step of the process. The secret, therefore, to achieving "free" productivity and quality improvement lies in knowing where to look for the nonvalue-adding time, how to know when we find it, and how to eliminate it from our processes.

Solving the Secret?

Time is the key. How is time invested in an endeavor? How we use time can be divided into five discrete segments:

1. Queue time
2. Preparation time
3. Value-adding time
4. Waiting time
5. Transfer time

These discrete time elements can be found in each step of any process. When we aggregate this time across the process, we derive *total process time.*

Let's examine each segment in two environments: manufacturing and administrative.

Queue Time. In a manufacturing shop floor environment, this is the time that material resides in queue at a manufacturing operation waiting for the operator to use it. This applies both for unattended automated operations, as well as for manned operations.

In the administration, queue time can be represented by the in-basket. Work that is staged in the in-basket is sitting in queue awaiting subsequent action.

Preparation Time. On a manufacturing shop floor, preparation represents set-up time, the time required to prepare an operation or machine to manipulate the material waiting in queue in front of the operation.

In the administrative realm, preparation activities can range from acquiring needed forms or supplies, to signing onto the computer system and bringing up an application appropriate to taking subsequent action on in-box items. We could also be preparing for a meeting or analyzing the elements required to reach a decision.

Value-Adding Time. In manufacturing, this equates to "run" time. We are now actually doing something to the material to transform it into a salable product.

In administration, we are now acting on an item from the in-basket. We could also be interacting and contributing in a team situation or making a decision.

Waiting Time. In manufacturing, we would typically stage material, at an operation, once we have concluded run time requirements. Material would be staged awaiting transfer to the next operation in the process.

In the administrative area, waiting time is symbolized by the out-basket. We have finished an administrative action and place a form in the out-basket, awaiting transfer to the next department or individual required to process the form. This could be an approval action in which an item has to travel through a cycle before being approved.

Transfer Time. In manufacturing, this is the time required to move material from one manufacturing operation to the next operation in the production process. Typically, material is moved into queue at the next operation.

In the administrative realm, this is the time required to move an item from one out-basket to another in-basket.

Transfer time can occur across considerable distances. Material, forms, documents, and people can be located floors apart, buildings apart, and geographically apart.

Of all these time segments, only the value-adding time segment contributes value to the outcome we are trying to achieve. Each of the other time segments represents some form of overhead. The 5-percent rule indicates that, of these time segments, the value-adding time segment consumes no more that 5-percent of the time invested in a process, and the other time segments consume the remaining 95 percent. Thus we know where to look for nonvalue-adding time and how to know it when we find it.

What remains is to eliminate it. Elimination of nonvalue-adding time can range from simply reorganizing where people sit to reengineering products and processes. There is no feasible way to present specific actions that, when applied, will result in the elimination of nonvalue-adding time. There are too many possibilities to consider. Instead, you will find presented in this book the process by which you can transform existing processes into response-managed ones in which nonvalue-adding time has been greatly reduced.

Suffice it to ask here, what would happen if, using existing labor and machine resources, you could significantly reduce the 95-percent component of your manufacturing or administrative processes. What impact would this have upon real productivity, profitability, capacity, and customer response levels? The impact on an organization has been recognized by response-managed competitors. They will employ the rule to improve all internal functions. The goal for a response-managed organization is to attain a level of performance such that most activities occur primarily in value-adding time. The other time segments can rarely be entirely eliminated, but they can be reduced to insignificance.

❑ ❑ ❑

The Security of Knowing

Organizations have to deal with ever changing situations. How we respond is often a function of the ways in which we evaluate the requirements of our response and determine what action to take. In too many instances, this process can be confusing. An unfortunate illustration of what can often happen is found in the story of four people.

This is the story about four people:

Everybody, Somebody, Anybody, and Nobody.
There was an important job to be done
and Everybody was asked to do it.
Everybody was sure Somebody would do it.
Anybody could have done it, but Nobody did it.
Somebody got angry about that
because it was Everybody's job.
Everybody thought Anybody could do it,
but Nobody realized that Everybody wouldn't do it.
It ended up that Everybody blamed Somebody

In the response-managed organization, energy is devoted to continually improving response capabilities. To focus this energy, we must understand what drives response. What trigger event tells us that we have to respond? The answer consists of one word: need. Unless there is a need for what we each individually do or a need for what we collectively do as an organization, we have no reason to respond. Need equates to demand for our products or services. In the response-managed organization, demand is the trigger that calls the individual or organization to action.

Demand can come from sources outside the organization, or from sources within the organization. *Outside* demand usually reflects customer- or market-driven need. Those who buy our products or services want some quantity of one or the other. The needed quantity represents a demand trigger, which signals the need to respond. How we respond to this need places a demand on resources within the organization. So outside demand creates *internal* demand. The ability of our internal resources to respond to external demand determines our level of performance as a response-managed organization.

The need to respond to demand is not peculiar to the response-managed environment. Indeed, need is the foundation for most business endeavors. What separates the response-managed organization from more traditional organizations is how they respond and how quickly they respond. The defining characteristic is *balance—*

among functions, individuals, and resources—which provides the ability to consistently respond to external demand. This level of response is achieved when internal resources are organized for the purpose of responding quickly to external demand. In other words, the organization and its internal processes are *demand-driven*. Internal processes are demand-driven and balanced.

Once a process—any process—is organized in such a way that the individual steps making up the process are demand-driven and the work flow through the process is balanced, the capacity of that process ceases to vary. In a balanced, demand-driven process, capacity is not a variable. In this situation, capacity can be reliably stated as equaling some unit of performance within a specified, repeatable time period.

If the process is administrative in nature, then it might be appropriate to express its level of performance as so many forms per hour. For a manufacturing process, we can express capacity, for example, as so many widgets per hour. The unit of time may vary, and the unit of productivity may vary. But, once a balanced relationship is established, the ratio of units of production within some unit of time will not vary.

When this fact is combined with the 5-percent rule, productivity and efficiency reach optimum levels and costs stabilize to become constants. A balanced, demand-driven process that is performing in value-adding time represents the ideal. This level of performance cannot be surpassed. Once reached, all resources associated with the process are performing to optimum. Achieving this level of performance relates future productivity measures to time. The balanced, demand-driven process can improve productivity either by reducing the time required to respond or by increasing the quantity of product or service provided in a unit of time. Time becomes the measure of productivity.

What does all of this have to do with "knowing"? Quite a bit. Traditional organizations devote much of their resources to dealing with uncertainty—typically uncertainty about their ability to consistently respond to ever-changing market pressures and demands. Each department within the organization strives to improve its individual ability to respond to outside pressure without regard to the needs of the overall organization.

Variance and the measurement of variance define our standard measures. Since we do not expect consistency in response, we invest heavily in collecting and quantifying our inconsistency. We call this variance reporting. We all do it. But why should we? What good is it to measure inconsistency if no attempt is made to eliminate inconsistency? *The issue is not to measure variance, but to eliminate it.*

What do we know once capacity ceases to be a variable? We know, with great precision, exactly what our productive capabilities are. We know how we are capable of responding to external demand. This knowledge has a positive influence on virtually every aspect of organizational activity.

For example: If we know our productive ability on the shop floor or administrative ability in the office, we can match this ability to demand with great precision. We *know* how long it will take us to respond to different levels of demand. We *know* if, when, and to what extent we will have to add additional shifts or work overtime to satisfy demand. We *know* what we need to establish stable production schedules which will be attained with great consistency. We *know* what our material requirements will be to support those production schedules. We *know* what machinery and equipment we will need, and when we will need it to support those production schedules. We *know* with a high-degree of certainty when those equipments and machines will require maintenance and can reliably schedule accordingly. We *know* how much inventory, if any, we will have to carry to satisfy typical customer demand. We *know* what response capabilities we require from our suppliers to meet our production schedules. We *know* what impact special sales or marketing promotions will have on our ability to respond. We *know* how to use our ability to respond rapidly and consistently to our advantage in distinguishing our organizations from our more traditional competitors. We *know* how to develop new products quickly. We *know* with a very high-degree of accuracy, exactly what our costs are throughout the organization. We *know* our customer service response capabilities. We *know* our administrative response capabilities.

We know what our capabilities are to respond to any and all competitive issues. We are secure in our knowledge of how to best use our resources to maintain this position.

5

The Codependent
Customer Chain

Who Is the Boss?

In today's quality lexicon, the customer is "the boss," the ultimate judge of whether we succeed or fail. The total quality management approach extends the concept of "customer boss" to include both the traditional external customer (who consumes our product or service) and an internal customer (one of our peers who is directly affected by what we do inside our company or organization).

This belief—that the customer is the boss—is very strongly held. During a visit to a client's office, I noticed a large poster, prominently hung in the administrative lunch room. The poster boldly proclaimed "Who Is the Boss" and provided the following answer to that question:

Who Is the Boss?

This is one question you can ask a thousand working people and never get the right answer. The question is: WHO IS THE BOSS?

Whether a man sweeps floors for a living or is president of the largest corporation, there is only one boss. In all cases ...THE BOSS IS THE CUSTOMER.

Never forget that THE CUSTOMER IS THE BOSS. He pays all salaries and decides if a business succeeds or fails. THE BOSS buys and pays for everything we will ever own. He pays our bills in the exact same proportion to the treatment he receives from us. Treat THE BOSS badly...customer, public—all the same person...and he will put us out of business. THE BOSS can fire everyone in the company simply by spending his money with someone else.

Our responsibility to ourselves and our commitment to our company is to remember:

THE CUSTOMER IS THE BOSS

Is there anything wrong with this picture? How can any reasonable person question such sentiments? The fact is, these sentiments might be good or not so good. I suggest that the relationship implied by the concept of THE CUSTOMER AS BOSS is unhealthful to continued prosperity and unproductive.

Let's analyze this idea from a response-managed perspective. The use of the word *boss* to describe the customer implies that those who serve "the boss" are in some manner subordinate to "the boss." This is consistent with the image conveyed in the poster: The boss has the authority to hire and fire subordinates. A condition of inequality is suggested, in which the supplier of products or services is implicitly less equal than the buyer, who is "the boss."

Is this an accurate depiction of the relationship between business associates, inside or outside an organization? Does this relationship imply that those serving the boss should assume a subservient posture in this relationship? Should the wishes of the boss be questioned? Or would this be considered a challenge to the boss's authority?

The response-managed organization redefines this implied relationship. All the notions, from the initial idea of a dominant boss–subordinate relationship to the idea of the boss always being right, are all nonproductive and unhealthful approaches to this relationship.

Who are the customers? They are our business partners, mutually dependent on each other. Instead of striving to ensure the success of the other, we should be seeking a partnership in which neither is dominant. We should seek ways to share resources, to expand markets, to improve quality (however we define it), to partner in such a way so that each derives equitable benefit from the relationship.

Is the customer always right? What if a customer wants something that they do not need or that will not benefit them, *and you know it.* Is the customer still the boss? Should or would a true "quality" supplier just agree with the customer because he or she is the boss?

The winning relationship is one in which the customer is our partner, not our boss. It is a relationship in which we and our customer share information to better ensure that we are each contributing to our relationship and our mutual benefit.

Ultimately, we are all both customers and suppliers. As suppliers, should we want to be treated any differently by our customers than we treat our suppliers when we are the customers? The biblical reference of "do unto others as you would have others do unto you" comes to mind. Why should this not apply to our business relationships with suppliers and as customers?

It is time for a reality check. Certain readers may say "Right, but you obviously never met some of our customers." Granted. Not all customers are actively seeking a partnership relationship with their suppliers, nor are they necessarily seeking a relationship in which they interact as equals. Nor, for that matter, is the idea of a coequal trading partner relationship agreeable to many, if not most, companies. It is certainly nonexistent for many companies, particularly those who dominate their industry or dominate a specific product type. During their period of dominance, many of these companies expect to be treated not as equals to anybody, but as organizations that are unarguably superior to all others. Several such companies come readily to mind: one in computing, another in auto manufacture, and yet another in farm equipment.

I *am* suggesting, however, that companies exhibiting this attitude are thriving on borrowed time. Certainly this has proven true of the three companies just alluded to (you identify the companies on your own). Such an air of superiority will definitely leave an organization vulnerable to attack from a determined response-managed strategy. These organizations will also be vulnerable to attack by "lesser" organizations that decide not to accept a position as inferiors. They are especially vulnerable if attacked by those joined in a codependent response-managed chain.

Market arrogance can prevail only in the absence of vigorous effective competition. Eventually, those who are convinced of their superiority are confronted with customer reality, which expresses itself in the statement, "Your products just don't measure up." They may not measure up in quality, diversity, technology, cost, features, or any one of many other parameters.

"Breakthrough": Our Customer
Wants What We Want

In the codependent customer chain, each buyer/seller entity is one link joined to the other links in the service of the final customer. The nature of codependency is such that each member of the chain strives to ensure the continued success of every other member of the chain. Each member of the chain is not only in a state of continual individual improvement, but also engaged in a cooperative continual improvement relationship with other chain members. The end goal is to establish a state of cooperative improvement from which each link profits.

What is the starting point on this path to becoming a link in a codependent chain? It can be found in the phrase, "Our customers want exactly the same things that we do." This statement defines a fundamental truth that is the cornerstone of any sound business improvement program. Is this different from the prevailing emphasis placed on customer satisfaction? Yes!

It has become common practice to direct our energies toward the customer, who has become a focal point for quality programs. "We want to ensure that we provide our customers with the highest quality products and services" is a sentiment loudly proclaimed in most mission statements. It provides the basis for embarking on total quality management programs or other quality-oriented programs. These programs usually recognize the two categories of customer we have identified: the internal customer, the person or department that will next handle what "I" am working on or that is directly affected by it, and the external customer, the one who buys our products or services.

Even though a focus, the customer, has been established, many organizations still struggle to more precisely define a purpose for their programs. The *customer* and *quality* are words that by themselves do not provide enough precision to adequately define a competitive program. Yet, many organizations seem to embark on quality improvement programs without really knowing why they were doing so or what the program means. "It was the right thing to do." "Our competitors forced us to respond." "We just knew that we could improve upon the way we were doing things." These are some of the reasons given for these programs.

Quality and cost are, by themselves, not enough to support and sustain programs aimed at improving each. An organization can produce or provide a 100-percent quality product priced below the competition's, yielding a high profit margin, and still fail if not enough customers are buying the product or service. Buggy whips and CB radios come to mind.

The addition of time to the equation improves our ability to compete but still does not provide an answer to the question, "What do we do next?" An organization decides to adopt a quality/cost/time improvement program. Where do they start? What do they do next? What are the objectives of their program? Why, where, and when do they act? What do they do when they act? What actions will allow them to become a link in a codependent chain? Enter the breakthrough principle: "Our customers want exactly the same things that we do." Here is the universal answer to the question of why, where, when, and what. The answers derive from what both we and our customers want. This premise lies at the heart of a response-managed competitive program.

Why is this a fundamental truth? What we and our customers want will change over time. Change will be driven by events in technology, methods, markets, practices, and other influences. Change will be constant: The product or service attributes that we want will change and what our customers want will change. What will not change is the fact that our customers will invariably want the same things that we want.

If we recognize this principle, then we can establish a foundation for our quality/cost/time improvement program. We will, with great precision, be able to determine where we have to take action, why we have to take that action, when to take the action, and what action to take.

Let's examine *some* of the things which "we" could want and determine if our customers might also want the same things.

To Improve Our Competitive Position. Usually organizations strive to improve their competitive position; they try to find ways to distinguish themselves from their competition. "Buy from us because we can provide...and our competitors can't." We certainly do not want to be in the position of the competitor who can't.

We must ask ourselves, "Do our customers want to improve *their* competitive positions?"

To Increase Market Share.   Part of our desire to improve our competitive position is the desire to increase market share. Very few, if any, organizations have established programs aimed at reducing market share. This is not the same as reaching a decision to withdraw from a market.

Most companies are striving to find ways to improve their penetration of markets, to expand or retain their market share. In some instances, the ability to retain existing market share is the equivalent of increasing that share. This is especially true when market share can be retained in the face of vigorous competitive pressures.

We must ask ourselves, "Do our customers want to increase *their* market share?"

To Improve the Quality of Our Customers.   Customers can be divided into two other categories: those whom we enjoy doing business with and those whom we endure. Another way to look at this difference is to recognize that some customers have only one priority, cost. All their buying decisions are based on how much a product or service costs. These customers see the buying decision as basically a commodity type of purchase. There is another type of customer, one who makes demands on our abilities. This customer expects quality, service, and response from their suppliers. This customer is usually willing to pay a premium to receive these attributes. This customer will be loyal to the supplier who can satisfy their requirements.

This second type of customer will usually be a company that has decided to become "world class" and understands the value associated with quality, service, performance, and so forth. This customer will have realized that the price of purchased goods or services is very different from the cost of those goods or services. More and more, the better customers are making new demands—demands that pertain to value-added services and not just to cost. Companies who are not able to quickly respond to these demands are losing these quality customers to their competitors, who are able to respond.

World-class organizations will also realize this difference. These organizations will target their competitive efforts toward other world-class organizations or toward the better customers, leaving the commodity customers to the competition.

We must ask ourselves, "Which companies do our customers wish to do business with, the commodity or value-added customers?"

To Improve Profits. When we attempt to increase our competitive advantage, to increase market share, and to expand our base of quality customers, one objective is to improve profits. Most organizations desire to improve profits. Rarely does an organization decide to actively work towards reducing profits.

We can ask ourselves, "Do our customers also wish to increase their profits?"

To Increase Inventory Turns. Another way to improve profits is to increase inventory turns, whose benefits most companies understand. Increasing inventory turns affects the dollars that they have to commit to inventory, the mix of items in inventory, the space required for inventory, the carrying cost of inventory, the quality of material in inventory, and the loss of inventory to obsolescence or engineering change. These are only some of the benefits of increasing inventory turns.

We should ask ourselves, "Do our customers also want these benefits?"

To Reduce Purchase Lead Time. The greater the delivery lead time of a material, the greater is the risk associated with its purchase. With extended lead times, we invariably order based on projected demand, on a forecast. Since we can all agree that the forecast will be wrong, we can also agree that we will be investing dollars to purchase material that we do not really need.

Most organizations would prefer to be able to order material when they actually need it, and to know that their supplier will be able to respond quickly to that need. In a response-managed organization, the ability to respond to changing market demands is ultimately determined by the ability of their suppliers to provide the raw materials needed to support their response systems.

We must ask, "Would our customers like us to provide them with short purchasing lead times?"

To Reduce Purchase Lot Size. Purchase lot size is also associated with the ability of a supplier to respond. When our suppliers can respond quickly to our needs, then we do not have to establish buffers—safety stock—in case they are not able to respond. If we desire to reduce purchasing lead time and to increase inventory turns, we must be able to also reduce purchasing lot sizes. This is the trend of the future: more frequent deliveries of fewer items per delivery.

We must ask, "Would our customers like to reduce the lot size of the orders they place with us?"

To Order Based on Need Not on Forecast. Can a truly competitive organization afford to purchase supplies primarily on the basis of a forecast? Increasingly, companies are saying no to this question. Forecasts are always wrong.

Forecasts force us to order greater quantities of material than we actually need, less frequently than is desired, and with less accuracy than is necessary to support required customer service levels. Since we buy raw materials to create products that we hope our customers will buy, our customers and competitors establish the market response time expected for products. Our ability or inability to respond within this market-driven response fence determines the amount of finished goods inventory we need to buffer ourselves against our inability to respond. How can we get out of this trap? We must be capable of responding within the required response fence. One requirement of this response level is the ability to place orders based on actual demand and not on forecast.

We must ask, "Would our customers prefer to order based on forecast or on their actual demand for our products?"

To Improve Our Inventory Mix. For our customers to reduce order lot size, shrink order lead time, and increase inventory turns, they have to be able to improve the typical inventory mix. Typically, in spite of our best efforts, the mix of items in inventory is not equal to our expectations. No matter how sophisticated our forecasting systems, the customer seems to order products that are different from the ones we have on our shelves. (This is due to the finest espionage system ever created, the one used by our customers to find out, with great precision, exactly what we have in inventory. This information is needed so that the customer will know what *not* to order.) Companies would love to be able to improve the mix of products in inventory—to achieve a mix of products that are actually needed now.

A response-managed organization recognizes the benefits possible from establishing a proper mix of items. The response-managed organization will focus considerable resources towards achieving this objective. After all, the time invested in acquiring and managing the wrong stuff detracts from time that could be invested profitably. The response-managed organization would not allow time to be invested in this manner.

We can ask ourselves, "Which of our customers does not want to have the correct mix of items in inventory?"

To Reduce Paperwork. As companies improve response systems and capabilities, they find a need also to decrease the amount of paperwork associated with day-to-day tasks. Organizations that properly use currently available technology are also finding that they no longer need to maintain a paper trail to have an audit trail of business transactions. Better-quality business control systems and capabilities, such as those found in electronic data interchange (EDI) systems, provide a basis for reengineering many traditional paper-based business activities.

The result of reengineering is usually to eliminate much or even all of the paper involved in a specific activity. An excellent example of this can be seen in the purchasing arena. As business or trading partnership relationships replace the old adversarial relationship between supplier and buyer, the manner and content of the relationship changes. Purchase orders are replaced with production schedule releases. Traditional inventory transactions, such as the receiving and issuing of material, are replaced by transactions telling a system how much of an item was used, when and where, backflush transactions. Invoices are being replaced by EDI-generated remittance advice transactions, which are sent directly to the bank upon receipt of the material for which payment is being made. Numerous advantages and benefits await the organization that successfully reduces the administrative burden associated with day-to-day operating requirements.

We can ask, "How many of our customers want to increase the amount of paperwork required to continue to do business with us?

To Improve Efficiency. Traditionally, being efficient meant being cost-effective. We were efficient if we achieved a result in the most cost-effective way; we minimized labor, material, and overhead to the absolute minimum required for the task at hand. We even looked at how we used these resources and tried to find ways to achieve results more "efficiently."

Now, with our new-found emphasis on response-managed competition, efficiency takes on an added dimension: response. To be efficient means to perform a task in the shortest possible time, to be capable of responding to the ever-changing demands of our market place. The ability to respond becomes the primary focus, not necessarily reducing the labor required to achieve the response. By focusing on response, we are forced to utilize only that amount of labor required to achieve the desired response level. Attaining this level could require an increase or decrease in labor. If we become efficient in how we respond, we will also become efficient in how we use all of our resources—human, material, and overhead.

We must ask ourselves and our customers, "Do we wish to become more or less efficient than we are today?"

To Improve Quality.   No matter how they choose to determine or meas-ure quality, not many companies would say that their objective is not to improve quality. Improving quality is not the question; under-standing which quality to improve is. Do we strive to improve the quality of activities that have no affect on our ability to serve our customers? How do we determine where to begin our quality improvement process, and how do we prioritize areas of considera-tion? These questions are answered by understanding what our customers want.

Early in any transformation program, we must address the issues of perceived as well as real quality, as it exists in the eye of our customers, if we are to successfully compete in the response-man-aged arena. Our quality parameters have to be a reflection of our customers' expectation of quality. Remember that, to be competi-tive, it is not necessary for us to produce 100-percent quality products or services; it is, however, necessary for us to provide our customers with nothing less than 100-percent quality products and services.

> We must ask, "Which of our customers does not wish to receive top-quality service or products?"

To Improve the Ability to Respond to Our Customers' Needs.   Most com-panies today are dedicated to servicing their customers. They are seeking new ways to improve their ability to respond to the needs of their customers. We do this to gain a competitive advantage over our less capable peers. What we must never lose sight of is that we all are someone's customer. When we make a purchase, as the customer, do we desire the advantages just outlined? If we do, then isn't it probable that those who purchase our goods or services—our customers—also desire these same advantages?

Can we identify a final customer? Yes. It is the consumer of a product or service who is the last to use it exclusively for their own use. In some instances, the final customer may also provide products or services to their customers. An example of this would be consumable tooling in a hard goods environment or office supplies to support the day-to-day administrative functioning of an operation. Our final customer buys the product for use in performing an administrative function or perhaps for producing a component of a product which they then sell to their customers. This is a subtle distinction from the purchase of a component part, which is consumed in a product, which is then sold to yet another customer.

In the service sector, consulting services are a good example of a service or product consumed by a customer and not directly passed onto their customer. In this case, the customer using the consultant could benefit from that interchange by improving their ability to better respond to their external or internal customers. In other words, consulting services are directed at altering the internal activities of the purchasing organization, and the result of the alteration is a positive impact on customers who rely on the actions or services provided by the purchasing organization. The purchasing organization is the final customer of the consulting service.

Why should we care about this distinction between final customer and internal customer? In the final analysis, the success of the final customer determines our success. Our business fortunes are directly tied to the business fortunes of the final customer using our product or services. If the final customer is successful, then demand for our portion of the end product or service will continue. When the final customer is not successful, demand for those products or services required by the final customer will diminish.

Response-managed organizations seek to develop mutually supportive codependent business relationships with their suppliers and customers throughout the entire competitive chain.

Codependency and the Final Customer

If you supply a product or service to a customer,
ultimately your success depends not on your
ability to produce a quality product but
on the ability of your customer to produce
a quality product. STEVE LEVIT

We know that the success of our final customer directly affects our ability to become successful and to remain successful—

whether our products are proprietary or standard, commonly available ones.

Let's further examine the relationships between supplier and customers. When we provide a product or service to final customers for that item, our ability to continue to sell to those customers is a function of their success. Their success, in turn, is directly affected by their ability to positively affect the success of their customers. This chain continues until the final customer is identified.

See Figure 5.1. Supplier A supplies components to customer B. B supplies assemblies to C, who uses the assemblies in the finished product, which they sell to customer D. Customer D uses the product, but not to produce another product or as part of any product that they offer to their customers.

The success of A depends directly on the success of D. The success of D is directly affected by the ability of C to enhance their competitive position. If C is not able to assist their customer D in either sustaining or increasing D's competitive position in the market place, C runs the risk that D will lose market share to a competitor who is able to increase their penetration into D's market. If D's customer base diminishes and their sales go down, their purchases of products from C will also diminish. If demand for C's products goes down, then C will reduce the quantity of products they acquire from B. B, in turn, will pass this reduction in demand back to their supplier A.

So the continuing success of A depends on the ability of C to enhance the competitive position of D. To be successful, both C and D realize that their futures are inexorably linked and that their success will result from mutual cooperation. All other members of the chain—A, B, and C—together have a responsibility to, through

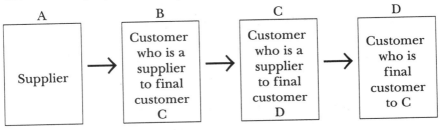

Figure 5.1. Tracking the final customer.

their actions, ensure the ability of C to assist D in increasing market share.

If B is unresponsive to their impact on the success of C in ensuring the competitive position of D, then B, C, and D will each suffer the consequences of B's actions. The same can be said of A with regard to their responsibility to support the ability of B to, in turn, support the next customer in the chain.

The existence of this chain suggests a new approach to how business is managed and conducted. It is not enough just to consider the impact of our actions on our immediate customer, that is, A on B. Such a narrow approach may make us vulnerable to an attack on D, to which we will be unable to respond. We must begin to develop a national business strategy that recognizes the entire customer chain as one process dedicated to ensuring the happiness and success of the final customer. All product- or service-providing organizations that participate prior to the final customer have to cooperate toward ensuring the success of their mutual final customer. They are codependant on each other in the achievement of this objective.

What happens when our product is proprietary, we are the only source of supply? Can we rely on this position as a safe haven in the modern global arena? If our business objectives are short term, with no concern for continuing success, then the answer is probably yes. If, however, our objectives are long term, the answer is no. If the supplier of a proprietary product or service is not able to participate in the ongoing success of their customers, eventually the customers will adopt one of several options: They will find substitute products. They will reengineer to utilize different products. They will encourage the establishment of competitive suppliers. Or they will seek every opportunity to drop this product and replace it with one that does not require the proprietary component.

In the future, most organizations will not be willing to endure the burdens imposed by "bad" suppliers. This situation is increasingly evident in the actions of the many so-called "better" companies as they seek to secure their competitive position in the new global economy. Codependency will define the business climate in future global markets. Those who can accept the challenge of codependency will succeed, and those who insist on maintaining a position of unilateral authority will fail in these markets. It will also be very difficult for new companies to break into an established codependent chain. New companies will have to find new reasons to be included in these chains. Typically, codependent chains will be linked by bonds that extend throughout all levels of the chain member organizations.

Each member of the codependent chain performs two roles: that of buyer and that of seller. The only exception to this rule is the final customer in the chain, who is a buyer only. Good buyers will buy only from good sellers; good sellers will sell only to good buyers. The strength of this relationship is the mutual support that each link in the chain provides to every other link in the chain.

Not only is each link strong by itself, but that individual strength is amplified through the relationships formed with the other links in the chain, the other codependents.

The codependent relationship is nurtured by response-managed organizations, who recognize the attributes associated with response as providing the elements of mutual support required by chain members.

Codependency and the Internal Customer

Let's apply the principle of codependency to internal customer relationships: In a codependent supplier/buyer chain, each member depends on the others for their individual and collective success; all are focused on the success of their final customer.

Can we apply this principle to the internal operations of individual members of the chain? The principle implies a cooperative, mutually supportive relationship among business entities. In other words, a group of organizations or individuals work in concert to achieve a common goal. Ideally, the members of the chain are linked together to form a high-performance team. This teamwork characterizes the relationships among member organizations as well as the relationships among individuals involved with the internal operations of each member of the chain.

Can we accomplish this kind of teamwork? Not only can we, but we must.

The internal workings of any business entity is comprised of a collection of codependent functions and departments. These entities are linked together in much the same way as the members of a codependent chain.

In the manufacturing arena, no individual function or department can effectively function isolated from the rest of the organization. Each function affects every other function in varying degrees and each function is in turn affected by every other function. The same can be said for service industry operations: the same state of codependency exists between functional departments. The success of an enterprise is therefore directly affected by the success of the relationship between these codependent functions. For the codependent organization, the final customer is the organization itself.

What are the requirements for a successful cofunctioning organization? There are five distinct requirements:

1. Each department has to realize that it does not stand alone but is instead a link in a chain of events culminating in the success of the organization.

2. Each department has to become aware of the other elements of the chain in which it is a link.

3. Each department has to understand the purpose of the chain and how the chain functions.

4. Each department has to understand how its actions affect the other links in the chain and how it is influenced by the actions of other links in the chain.

5. Departments have to work together to achieve organizational objectives. Cross-functional teams are formed in support of this end.

The codependent organization is made up of cross-functional teams, some of which are permanent and others of which are temporary, having been formed in response to specific short-term issues.

Individuals may find themselves on more than one team at a time. Decision criteria are developed in a team environment with final decisions being made either by the team, when so empowered, or by the person who initiated the team.

A properly constituted team environment ensures that decision support criteria consider the impact of a decision on each member department impacted by the decision. This type of team environment will usually produce higher-quality decisions than are available through more traditional methods. Quality improvements result from the diversity of expertise and experience contributed by individual team members to the decision. Not only will decisions be reached more rapidly, they will be of higher quality and will be implemented more rapidly than those made unilaterally by an individual or department.

Response-managed organizations are organized into *teams*, or collections of individuals associated with specific decisions. Team members are placed in close proximity to each other to facilitate immediate and effective communication among them. In this environment, they can answer questions quickly, resolve issues and difficulties, and, most importantly, serve customers—both internal and external customers.

How many times have you called a company for information and found yourself shunted from person to person, from department to department, in an attempt to find just the right individual to respond to your needs? How much did you like this experience (assuming you received a satisfactory response to your needs)? How often were you frustrated in your attempts to obtain what you thought was basic information? How often have you been told, "We will have to get back to you on this one"? As a customer, how do you feel about this kind of treatment? Would you rather endure such frustrations or receive an immediate, knowledgeable response? This is a foolish question, perhaps. Yet the latter is the exception and the former the rule.

Teams and teamwork (discussed in detail in Chap. 6, page 93) help to avoid such problems, an internal codependency provides a rationale for teams. Survival is the justification for teams, and increased profit is the benefit derived from them.

Time in a Codependent Chain

In the codependent chain the ability of each link to respond in support of each other link is vital to the success of the chain and of the final customer. Response becomes an underlying principle defining the way that competition will be waged. Those who will be able to improve their ability to respond to the needs of customers up to and including the final customer will prosper and be competitive. Those who are not able to meet this criterion will ultimately fail or be absorbed by those who have succeeded in this new competitive arena. The ability to respond is measured in units of time rather than in units of quality. We work to reduce the time it takes to perform operations. By reducing time we improve our ability to respond.

This improved ability to respond will eventually extend throughout an organization, affecting all operational departments. As each individual link in the chain improves their response capabilities, their ability to support both their upstream (customers) and downstream (suppliers) improves.

When the entire chain is responsive it becomes a formidable business entity that is capable of outpacing its competition in all areas of endeavor. Those who are members of a codependent chain will be so far ahead of their more traditional competition that they can expect to be accused of somehow "cheating."

The good news for those desiring to become response-managed organizations is the amount of time eligible to be eliminated. The bad news is how we traditionally use the available time. For almost ten years now, I have been aware of what I called the 5-percent rule. This rule is discussed in detail in Chap. 4, "Building Bridges to the Future: Developing Procedures." Simply put, the rule says that for most organizations, and across virtually all functions, no more than 5 percent of the time we invest toward achieving a business objective actually contributes to our attainment of the stated objective. Ninety-five percent of the time we invest is nonvalue-added time.

The response-managed organization sees this situation as an opportunity to establish a dominant competitive position among competitors. Those who are first to recognize the importance of time in achieving response and who proactively take steps to eliminate nonproductive time from their operations will fly past their competition.

When one competitor is suddenly confronted by another response-managed organization, the former may find it difficult or even impossible to catch up. Apart from the impact on market share which may not be recoverable, the response-managed organization will be moving and improving at a pace which continues to increase with experience.

The competitor trying to catch up is usually first learning to walk before running. But RMO firms are not running; they are flying. For competitors, the response gap widens considerably before it begins to narrow, if at all.

> This is not an area where it is safe to rely on an ability to catch up. Those who do may find that they have forever lost the opportunity to play in the new competitive arena.

The Ripple Factor

The concept of codependency obliges us to recognize the need for fundamental change in how industrial and governmental entities work together: Many companies are finding that they are falling victim to codependent events resulting from the ripple factor.

What is the ripple factor? As business needs change in a codependent chain, the changes ripple backward and forward along the chain. Individual ripples are not always of great significance, but the cumulative effect of the ripples becomes a tidal wave of change.

Most companies are not prepared to absorb the ripples. They attempt to respond to each ripple as an isolated event, aggressively resisting any urge toward significant, fundamental change in how they operate.

Attempts to treat each ripple effect as an isolated phenomenon, however, does not prepare an organization to deal with the inevitable tidal wave of change. Isolated phenomena do not usually become incorporated into an organization's strategy. The result is an organization that operates without the benefit of overall guiding principles—without a foundation on which to build a coordinated organizational response strategy.

These organizations will become losers in the emerging competitive battles. For them, the cumulative impact of the ripple effect will be chaos. Without a coordinated organizational strategy to guide them, each externally driven ripple will create an internal ripple within the organization. The internal ripples, in turn, will contribute to interdepartmental conflict. As each affected department seeks to cope with the impact of change in the absence of coordinating guidelines, each ripple effect carries the risk of chaos. Internal ripple effects result in the introduction of additional change until the cumulative effect is chaos.

We can easily identify those organizations who have entered a state of chaos. They become "finger-driven" entities: Every finger points away from the individual and his or her department. Problems are "their fault," never ours. "If only they had done something [or had not done something], we would not be in this position today."

The frequency of change is increasing. Technological growth, combined with advances in methods has created an environment where the pace of change is continually accelerating. As a result, the ripple effect is growing. What was a tidal wave of change in the decade of the 1980s will grow into *tsunami* proportions during the 1990s. So the longer we wait before adopting integrating corporate strategies aimed at transforming the organization into a coordinated, energized competitive entity, the harder it will be to respond to the coming tidal wave of change.

The ripple factor can also be applied to trading partner relationships. Response-managed organizations will have realized two things: (1) Their suppliers have a direct effect on their ability to respond to their customers. (2) Their ability to respond to customers has a direct effect on the customers' ability to respond to their customers, until we reach the end of the chain, the final customer.

As a case example, a corporation, with which I was familar, had a very aggressive sales force, which brought in record levels of business. As an emerging "world-class" company, they offered their customers acceptable delivery lead times. Demand grew; the future looked great.

Their customers were elated and based their business decisions on the availability of the materials they were purchasing from this world-class company. Their future also looked great.

The supplier then analyzed their ability to respond to the growing demand for their product. They found that, even by using all their resources, going to three shifts, adding an additional production line, they would not be able to deliver product within the promised lead time. Many of their customers would have to wait not the promised two weeks, but two months instead.

What to do? We surely did not want to stop Sales from doing their job. We could not afford the capital expense of adding capacity to handle what may only be a temporary increase in demand.

The company had to notify their customers that they would be unable to respond to their needs. Their customers, in turn, had to notify their customers that they would not be able to respond as promised. I did not inquire about the impact beyond this point in the chain.

This is one example of a ripple factor effect—the actions of one link in the codependent chain directly affecting the other links in the chain.

6
Reengineering for Response

Reengineering

Past success is not a guarantee of future prosperity
STEVE LEVIT

The transformation from a "traditional" organization to an RMO results from reengineering existing processes to transform them into response-oriented processes. It is now time to specifically apply the principles from the 5-percent rule, discussed in Chap. 4, to our existing processes.

By applying the 5-percent rule to our reengineering efforts, we are able to identify and eliminate response inhibitors from our organizations. Response inhibitors are discussed elsewhere in this chapter.

The 5-percent rule provides a foundation for our reengineer efforts. Improved response is the goal of our reengineering effort. The transformation process described in Chap. 2 outlines the steps required to successfully reengineer, first a demonstration or pilot process and then to expand that effort to reengineer an entire organization.

There are many obstacles which can stand in our way as we attempt to reengineer for response. One obstacle relates to the way in which people view themselves to be indispensable. I am reminded of the poem "Indispensable":

Indispensable
> When you're feeling so important
> And your ego is in bloom
> When you simply take for granted
> You're the wisest in the room
> When you feel your very absence
> Would leave a great big hole,
> Just follow these instructions
> They will humble any soul.
> Take a bucket filled with water
> Put your hand in to the wrist,
> Pull it out, the hole remaining
> Is how much you will be missed.
> Splash wildly when you enter,
> Stir a lot and splash galore.
> Then stop, and in a minute,
> It looks just like before.
> The moral of this story
> Is do the best you can
> Be proud, but please remember,
> There's no indispensable man.

Change and Response

Another obstacle is resistance to change. The idea of reengineering implies change. It is based on the premise that in the modern business world, change has become the only constant.

Changing is never easy, except for those for whom change has become the way of life.

For most of us, change is something to be resisted. We remain comfortable with what is and become uncomfortable when we consider what might be. "What is" represents the known. Through experience we develop our response to each situation that presents itself, and we become comfortable with that response. For example, we are very comfortable with the "self-evident fact" that light bulbs emit light. However, what if that theory were all wrong? What if an alternate theory were instead true?

Light vs. Dark

As an example, for years it was believed that electric bulbs emitted a substance or energy called light. Recent information, however, has proven otherwise.

Electric bulbs don't emit light; they suck dark. Thus we call these bulbs dark suckers. Dark Sucker Theory presents a number of basic theorems concerning the properties of dark. For example:

1. The speed of dark is greater than that of light.

2. Dark has greater mass than light.

The basis of Dark Sucker Theory is that electric bulbs suck dark. Take, for example, the dark suckers in the room where you are. There is less dark right next to them than there is elsewhere. The larger the dark sucker, the greater its capacity to suck dark. As with all things, dark suckers don't last forever. Once they are full of dark, they can no longer suck. This is proven by the black spot on a full dark sucker. A candle is a primitive dark sucker. A new candle has a white wick. You will notice that, after the first use, the wick turns black, representing the dark that has been sucked into it. Unfortunately, these dark suckers have a limited range.

There are also portable dark suckers. The bulbs in these units can't handle all the dark by themselves, and they must be aided by a dark storage unit. When the dark storage unit is full, it must be either emptied or replaced before the portable dark sucker can operate again.

Dark has mass. When dark goes into a dark sucker, friction from this mass will generate a certain amount of heat. It is commonly known that an operating dark sucker generates heat. The dark suckers with the greater capacities force the dark to travel through the impeding media at greater rates of speed, so they develop greater amounts of heat. Thus, it is not wise to touch an operating dark sucker.

Now to offer proofs of these theories stated.

First, dark is faster than light. If you were to stand in an illuminated room in front of a closed dark closet, then slowly open the closed door, you would see the light slowly enter the closet. But since the dark is so fast, you are not able to see the dark leave the closet.

Second, dark has more mass than light. If you swim just below the surface of a lake, you will see a lot of light. As you swim deeper and deeper, you notice it gets slowly darker and darker. This is because the dark sinks to the bottom of the lake and the light rises to the top.

Those accepting Dark Sucker Theory might be just as comfortable with their "self-evident fact."

We must always be ready for the challenge that change poses. The situation that causes us to respond can be either negative or positive, which does not matter since we have experienced it before and have accepted it as part of our way of life.

For those who have not yet adopted change as a way of life, the prospect of change can be terrifying. For these people, change represents disruption to their routine and uncertainty as to the outcome. Change exposes them to the risk of potential failure.

As long as this attitude persists, it becomes virtually impossible to progress beyond our immediate circumstance. Change is the price we must pay to improve on what is and transform it into what can be. *Change is the price of progress.*

For those who have adopted change as a way of life, change itself is eagerly sought because it is equated with improvement, and improvement is equated with enhanced self-interest. Improvement is the reason for change. Once we accept change as the only constant, the idea of change is incorporated into such traditional activities as goal setting. In the response-managed environment, goals are firmly cast in Jell-O™.

In practice, it is easy to make the transition from resistance, to change, to becoming a proponent of change. All that is required is change. The required change will result when we recognize that we are capable, individually as well as collectively as an organization, of doing better than we are currently doing. This is not a very great step to take. Who would insist on the alternative to such propositions as, "I/we cannot do better" or "I/we have attained a state of perfection that is no longer capable of improvement." Who would assign these traits to themselves or to the organizations by which they are employed? I have never met anyone who felt that they or their organizations were perfect and therefore not capable of improving. The path to accepting change thus requires that we become uncomfortable with some aspect of our individual or corporate condition.

Accepting change also means acknowledging that where we are today is the result of past actions. Past actions are the roads we followed before as our path to the present. As long as we stay on the same path, we can only arrive at the same destination. Our future will be the same as our past.

Once the decision is made to improve on the present, you have no alternative but to accept that you must now choose a different path than the one used to arrive at the present. If you elect a different destination than the present one, you must embark on a different path than the one that has guided you to the present.

How do you go about choosing a new path? To choose a new path, you must first know your new destination. Throughout the book, I have suggested a new destination, that of becoming a response-managed organization. The response-managed organization accepts change as the constant: Only change is permanent; everything else is temporary. To the response-managed organization, change implies steady growth and progress toward an ever evolving goal, which is defined by technology, market desires, customer requirements, and the development of new methods and standards of performance.

The response-managed organization has organized all company departments and functions to be capable of responding to this changing goal. Change is no longer a source of threat and discomfort, instead providing the excitement and exhilaration that comes from meeting difficult challenges head on and emerging victoriously.

Response Inhibitors

The journey toward becoming a response-managed organization will involve the transformation of existing activities into response-capable activities. This transformation process results from constantly asking such questions as: "Is what I am doing today making me more responsive?" or "Is the way I am doing things today making me more responsive?" We are seeking to identify response inhibitors so that we may take appropriate steps to remove them from our operations.

The answer to these questions is linked to another question: "Which actions can be identified as response inhibitors?" *Response inhibitors* are those functions, actions, processes, methods, and so forth that prevent us from attaining response-managed performance levels. To become response-managed, an organization must rethink existing activities to reduce or eliminate response-inhibiting actions.

When response inhibitors are introduced into an activity, regardless of the nature of that activity, its productivity is reduced. Response inhibitors tend also to be nonvalue-adding and most often contribute directly to operating overhead. This realization is important because not only do response inhibitors make us competitively weak (such as overhead), but they also affect our profit opportunities. We only have two options when dealing with overhead:

1. Pass it on to the consumer in the cost of a product.
2. Absorb it against our profit margins.

Which one would you choose for your organization?

Response inhibitors can be grouped into four broad categories (the four Ms): man, machine, materials, and methods. (The use of "man" is a convenience—it is not intended as a sexist approach or to exclude women.)

Typical response inhibitors associated with how we invest our labor resources are:

Man

Watching machines run	Poor morale
Looking for tools	Improper or inadequate training
Long machine setups	Too many meetings
Counting parts	Carrying heavy work pieces
Overproduction	Rework

Waiting for material to work on
Looking for forms, documents, supplies
Playing phone tag

Defects
Waiting for approvals

Trying to locate fellow workers

Attitudes

These are examples of response inhibitors that affect how effective we will be in performing daily activities.
Machine-related response inhibitors are:

Machine
Excessive breakdowns
Not flexible
Unavailable repair parts
Improperly maintained
Too far apart
Grouped in work center not in work line or cell
Improperly used

Difficulty in maintaining
Multipurpose
Dirty
Poorly lit
Wrong machine
Require long set-up times

It ain't broke, don't fix it!

There is an inexorable link between machines, maintenance, productivity, quality, and the ability of an organization to be responsive to market demands. This link is especially important in manufacturing. Without the machinery necessary to support manufacturing activities, manufacturing cannot be economically responsive to changing customer demand.

Response inhibitors can also affect how we manage material. Some examples include:

Materials
Temporary storage
Requires special handling
Transit time
Wait time
Rework
Space on shop floor for material

Overproduction
Annual physical inventory
Queue time
Scrap
Warehousing space
Excessive handling

Parts/material shortages	Inconsistent quality
Not to specification	Too many different parts
Excessive inventory, finished goods, and raw material	Not available when required

How we view and use material has a significant effect on how responsive the department or function relying on the material will be. The more response inhibitors are introduced into material-associated tasks, or to produce a product, the less responsive and productive that activity becomes.

Response inhibitors associated with operational methods are:

Methods

Transfer time	Queue time
Wait time	Preparation time
Function separation	Approval delays
Communication delays	Departmental segregation

How we use those resources and assets that are available to us in support of achieving performance objectives has a dramatic effect on how successful we will be in realizing our performance objectives. A response-managed organization will devote considerable energy towards the rapid assimilation of new methods and techniques that can contribute to increasing their ability to function as a rapid response organism.

Within our four categories we can identify 13 general types of nonproductive activities:

1. Overproduction
2. Step waste
3. Excessive material movement
4. Inventory levels
5. Unnecessary material processing
6. Unnecessary motion
7. Product defects

8. Capacity utilization
9. Communication inefficiency
10. Delays in response
11. Approval cycles
12. Decision chains
13. Confusion

Overproduction. This response inhibitor has a far reaching effect within an organization. At a minimum, overproduction contributes to each of the other nonproductive activities. Overproduction also imposes additional response-inhibiting conditions such as the need for:

- Extra space to store overproduced products.
- Additional overhead incurred in the production and storage of over produced products.
- Increased interest charges associated with the additional costs incurred to support overproduction.
- Added labor costs for the overproduction.
- Increased paperwork.
- Greater material acquisition costs.
- Unnecessary machine and tool usage, and productive capacity necessary to achieve overproduction.

Invariably, overproduction is used as an excuse to keep workers busy. "After all, we're not paying them to just stand around and do nothing, are we?" Overproduction is also a way to cover ourselves just in case we incur problems anywhere in our productive process. We confuse being busy with being productive.

We must realize that *production for any purpose other than to respond to real demands for products or services is a waste of resources.* It is better to let people sit idly than it is to have them produce products or provide services just to be busy. When we overproduce, we not only consume resources wastefully, but we further compound the situation by diminishing our ability to use those same resources for an alternative purpose that could be productive or beneficial.

Step Waste. This is the accumulation of nonvalue-adding activities associated with the performance of an individual step within a process. We can apply the 5-percent rule to define step waste. Step waste is found in virtually all administrative or productive functions within an organization. Within the 5-percent rule parameters, those time elements other than run time are response inhibitors.

Excessive Material Movement. The movement of material—from storerooms to the shop floor, from the shop floor back to storerooms, from receiving docks to warehouse locations, from one physical location to another, and from warehouse locations to shipping docks—is a common response-inhibiting activity in manufacturing organizations. The excessive movement of administrative support materials or decision support materials can be found in virtually all administrative and decision chain processes. In most organizations, excessive material movement also results in additional paperwork, such as pick lists, issue documents and receivers, approval slips, and general documentation. Excessive material movement also results when departments or manufacturing operations are geographically separated; when something is traveling between locations, it is not traveling to the customer.

Inventory Levels. Any discussion of inventory must begin with acknowledgment of the fact that inventory is usually held for valid reasons. Later in this chapter (page 90), it has been specifically discussed why inventory may be necessary to maintain competitive advantage. Yet companies fail to recognize why they maintain inventory levels in the first place, and they begin inventory reduction programs without taking these reasons into account. Taking this approach is a sure invitation to failure. Inventory itself is not the issue. Why we maintain inventory levels is the issue to deal with.

Having acknowledged the occasional need for some inventory, the next point is that inventory is overhead. It is a sinkhole for capital. It adds no value. If there is a benefit to inventory, it is what one manufacturer found when he eliminated WIP inventory: The noise level on the shop floor went up. So the only redeeming value of inventory is that it absorbs sound. Elsewhere in this chapter we discuss the relationship between response capabilities and inventory throughout an organization.

Many formulas exist for determining the most efficient way to accumulate inventory. In general these approaches are oxymorons; there is no efficient way to accumulate inventory. When we accumulate inventory, we diminish responsive abilities. We transfer the use of resources from support for immediate response to supporting inventory accumulation. Since, in most instances, we cannot do two things at the same time, investing in resources for inventory production prevents us from using the same resources to respond quickly to immediate demands.

Unnecessary Material Processing. Often, when design for manufacturability is not the governing principle of product design, a product will require unnecessary steps in the manufacturing activity. These steps may include such activities as filing material, repainting, assembly and disassembly of items, or compensating for worn tooling or fixtures.

Design engineering must begin to design for manufacture. Product design engineers must work with manufacturing people and with vendors as part of a new product design team. Products should be designed to be manufacturable using available manufacturing resources, or new manufacturing methods and/or resources should be developed concurrent with the product design effort.

If a process needs to be modified to accommodate the new product, the modification should be consistent with the principles of response-managed competition manufacturing principles. Response-managed processes include as few response inhibitors as is feasible.

Unnecessary Motion. Time invested in anything other than the attainment of particular goals or objectives delays the attainment of those goals or objectives. For example, too often we establish dedicated supply areas for objects—tool rooms, forms storage rooms, and so forth. Yet the motion necessary to acquire support materials, such as tooling, can inhibit response capability when tooling or supplies are not located as closely as possible to their point of need. The time a machine operator spends walking to get tooling or walking from one machine to another, or the time spent to get a "basket" of material to work on, may seem productive because the operator is in motion. Do not confuse motion with productivity. In reality, these times do not contribute to the attainment of our goal or purpose other than to increase a product's cost and reduce production capacity.

In manufacturing, machines should be placed together if they are to be operated by a single operator, so as to eliminate excess walking between them. Parts should be stored by the machine or by the routing step using the part.

The maintenance of part stocking levels is accomplished by material handlers responding to requests for resupply (Kanban) of production line locations. Operators keep the lines flowing.

In administrative or decision chains, support materials and personnel should also be grouped by purpose. For example, if a typical customer inquiry requires input from several departments, representatives from those departments could be grouped together rather than located in their respective departments. Close grouping allows for the immediate exchange of ideas and information among group members in response to outside requirements.

The more we physically or organizationally separate these people, the more we are inhibited from responding rapidly to varying situations.

Product Defects. Defective products must be identified, corrected, and accounted for in production scheduling. To accomplish this we usually put in place quality systems based on the inspection of product batches at predesignated points in a manufacturing process (routing). This allows us to determine that large quantities of product are defective. Once this is determined, we can either scrap the material or, having already invested labor and material, invest additional labor and possibly material to rework the product.

When we are aware that certain operations produce a known quantity of scrap, then our planning system, MRPII in many cases, will automatically plan larger manufacturing lot sizes to anticipate these failures and ensure that we receive the needed quantity of product at the end of the manufacture process. Thus, *we actually plan how much defective product to produce!*

Product defects are nothing more than response inhibitors. The time invested to make defective product is rendered unavailable for making good product. Defects therefore delay the production of "good stuff." Response-managed organizations strive to approach the unattainable goal of zero defects in all organizational activities. Within a manufacturing process, each operator is responsible for ensuring the quality of each part, each time, for each operation. Anything less inhibits the company's ability to respond.

Capacity Utilization. Capacity often equals response. To become competitive we must be capable of rapidly responding to whatever challenges our markets present over time. In this pursuit, the capacity to perform becomes the single greatest asset or obstacle in achieving competitive advantage. If we can increase capacity, we will also greatly increase productivity and quality simultaneously.

The way to increase capacity is to design processes capable of providing both elements concurrently. In manufacturing, one measure is to recognize that productive capacity cannot exceed the capacity of the slowest machine or step in the process. This point is often overlooked in traditional capacity planning. Traditionally, the unit of capacity is machine utilization and each machine is an island by itself. In this environment, similar machines are grouped into work centers with each machine identified as a workstation, where capacity is based on the ability of the work-center to process a manufacturing batch of material. Lot sizes are usually large, with a direct correlation between computed optimum lot size and set-up time. This is the environment we identified when we discussed "Step Waste." As in that instance, about 95 percent of the manufacturing cycle time found in a typical routing is waste time. If we are to be competitive, we must eliminate this waste time.

We must begin to view manufacturing activity not as a series of batch operations, but instead as a continuous process through which product flows instead of being staged in queues. As the waste time inhibitor is reduced or even eliminated, productive capacity increases on a one-to-one basis. For every hour of wasted time eliminated, we gain a corresponding hour of productive time. This increase in capacity (productivity) is realized *without increasing labor or machine overhead.*

When a response-managed process replaces an inventory-based process, using the 5-percent rule, capacity is increased and process cycle time is reduced. Once we remove the response inhibitors from the process, we are able to consider reducing inventories without incurring the risk of missed shipments.

Communication Inefficiency. We can usually identify many response inhibitors within our communication systems. The geographic separation between departments, the departmental separation of functions, long-distance methods of communication (phone, fax, electronic mail, and the like), or virtually any form of communication that is not immediately face-to-face will inhibit the ability to respond.

This is not to say that face-to-face communication by itself is automatically productive because the parties involved are able to present each other with their views on a topic. There is a difference between communication and dialogue. We frequently establish some level of dialogue, but we rarely communicate. (This distinction is expanded on in greater detail elsewhere in the book.) Dialogue can, however, serve to mitigate the inhibiting affect of communication inefficiency.

Delays in Response. The decision-making process we employ to reach conclusions allowing a response to varying situations will either inhibit or enhance our ability to respond quickly to those situations. Too often, response delays result from the accumulation of other response inhibitors such as unnecessary motion, movement, processing steps, or communication efficiency. As we delay response to situations and conditions that cry out for rapid resolution and response, we further inhibit our ability to respond effectively to those situations.

This condition results from the expectation that situations requiring a response are usually not static. They are dynamic. They evolve over time. The longer we take to respond to a situation, the greater the risk that our response will be to the situation before it evolved into something different. In other words, our response may not be appropriate to the situation as it exists at the moment of our response.

Once we fall into this trap, it may be very difficult to recover. Unless we can shorten our response time, we will always be dealing with what used to be, instead of what is. The further removed we become from what is, the greater the difficulty in developing an appropriate response that addresses or alleviates the condition requiring the response in the first place.

Approval Cycles.   The process of action approval can include many steps and actions that inhibit our ability to respond. Many organizations remove approval authority from the department or individual immediately involved in the situation requiring approval. Response to a need is delayed while the validity of the response is evaluated throughout the approval cycle.

In typical organizations, which are arranged vertically by department or function, approval cycles can take days, weeks, or months. Often, we exacerbate this condition by forming teams to develop reports, which are then evaluated and reviewed by others outside the team, to determine if an action should be authorized.

Decision Chains.   These are similar to approval cycles. In most situations, the decision cycle entails most of the response inhibitors just discussed. We tend to distribute decision-making authority across multiple departments, without providing a means for representatives from those departments to convene to influence those decisions. We strive to buffer ourselves from bad decisions by seeking consensus approval for action.

Consensus is by itself beneficial because it implies cross-functional interaction for common benefit. This is good. How we achieve consensus is the issue. Response-managed organizations will establish a responsive process. They live by an imperative to respond by reaching high-quality decisions quickly. The less capable, nonresponse-managed organization will employ decision processes that include many response inhibitors. These pose the same dangers as found in inhibited response and approval cycles; the decision reached is no longer appropriate for the situation being decided. "What was" is being decided, instead of "what currently is."

Confusion. It is just by coincidence that this response inhibitor is number 13. However, this is a most appropriate designation. Confusion is by itself a significant response inhibitor as well as the inhibitor which causes many of the preceding inhibitors to arise. I am forever amazed at the level of controlled chaos which appears to pervade so many organizations. Confusion is the result of many factors; our information systems, methods of communication, internal procedures, organizational structure as displayed in an "org chart," geographic separation between business entities and technologies, to name a few. The difficulty with confusion is that often we do not realize that we are operating in a confused manner, indeed we may be convinced that our actions are the very model of organization and efficiency. By way of illustration, I am reminded of a situation which I encountered while discussed total quality maintenance with a VP of operations and his plant engineer. The gist of the conversation was their inability to understand why whenever they attended maintenance seminars or conventions their contemporaries all spoke of unacceptable low maintenance productivity, typical "wrench" time estimates around 30 percent of the available time. Their maintenance people were so efficient that they did not even require supervision. Each crafts person carried a stack of maintenance work orders in their tool boxes. When they finished one job, they moved on to the next job on their list, they were *always* busy. Why, they were so dedicated that they even repaired their own printed circuit boards when they failed, even though their maintenance people were not trained in electronics. There is more, but this is enough. These people were obviously confused. They completely missed the point. To them, efficiency was defined as busy. As long as their maintenance people were every busy, they were efficient. They were so efficient that they could never catch up with their work load. They completely lost sight of the purpose of maintenance which is to ensure uninterrupted quality production during the production cycle. This objective could never be achieved until they realized that the work orders which their maintenance people carried in their toolboxes were themselves response inhibitors. They each represented a situation in which some aspect of their productive processes were operating at less than optimum or not at all.

A state of confusion is frequently found in the software systems which we use to manage our companies. When you take evaluate systems such as MRPII, you frequently find that they do odd things, or do not perform what should be intrinsic functions. Close investigation of this phenomenon will reveal that the system designers developed their system to respond to the specific needs of their customer base. As a result, their systems operate exactly in the way which their customers wanted without regard to the quality of that approach. Customers can and usually do request that their systems reflect the way in which their customers wanted without regard to the quality of that approach. Customers can and usually do request that their systems reflect the way in which they *currently* do things. As a result, some truly bizarre capabilities are developed and embedded in software packages. Now, a very curious thing happens. The presence of these bizarre features becomes the justification for transforming these features into system benefits. This is often stated as "well, why would you question how we do this, this is the way our customers do it." What are some examples; how about the ability to close a work order before the steps in its associated routing are closed? That's a good practice, after all, if we completed the work order we must have completed the steps right! One would wonder why we bothered with the routing in the first place. Or our system creates a pick list for inventory items associated with a work order. We enhanced our system to allow the user to issue the entire pick list with only one issue transaction. Isn't that great! Perhaps, but what happens if there are a few, two or three, exceptions in a pick list that contains many items? Do I now have to enter each line item on the pick list individually because of the few exceptions? I have seen systems respond to this situation in several ways; one is yes, it is then necessary to enter each item separately, another is to allow the entire pick list to be entered with one transaction and to then allow the user to go in to the system and correct the exceptions. Wow, that's great. First we are allowed to enter known incorrect information into the system, and this is considered as good because we can go in after the fact and correct that information. I suggest this is a good indicator of confusion in action. To first allow known errors to be entered, justified by the ability to correct afterwards completely misses the point, this is backwards. Known incorrect information should never be entered into a system. Instead, provision should have been provided to enter the exceptions and then to do an issue for the remaining items with one transaction.

Operating from a state of confusion can cause us to perform unnatural acts while believing in the absolute validity of those acts.

As you can see, response inhibitors share a common element: time. In varying degrees, they all relate to how time is invested to achieve a specific purpose, to the impact of time on performance. The ability to respond is inexorably linked to time. Response implies speed, and speed is measured in units of time. Response inhibitors thus become any action, condition, or situation that injects time into an activity beyond what is optimum for the activity. Anything that prevents us from responding to legitimate business issues—whether internal or external, customer- or market-driven—can be categorized as a response inhibitor.

Inventory Is Not the Problem

Has your company ever adopted an inventory reduction program? Do you know of any companies that have tried such a program? Why? The thought is good; the result can be deadly. Inventory is not the problem. The problem is why the inventory is there.

We can find many reasons to have inventory. Of these, there is one constant, the relationship between our ability to respond and inventory. Inventory *always* reflects an inability to respond:

When we cannot adequately respond to customer delivery expectations, we maintain finished goods inventory as a buffer against these expectations.

When we cannot schedule material requirements effectively, and/or when our suppliers cannot respond within short lead times, we buffer ourselves against this inability to respond with raw material inventory.

When we do not use our manufacturing resources efficiently or when we do not understand how to utilize our real productive capacity, we buffer ourselves against these deficiencies with work-in-process inventory.

We always use inventory as a buffer against our inability to respond. In this context, inventory is "good" because it allows us to continue functioning effectively. Without this buffer, most companies could not meet day-to-day operating demands. The description of inventory as "good" is, of course, conditional on the absence of other options.

Attempts to reduce inventory without first dealing with why the inventory is there in the first place are very high-risk pursuits. Those attempting such solutions incur the risk of successfully reducing inventory levels only to run smack into one or more of the problems that caused us to maintain the inventory in the first place.

Isn't this what we wanted to do anyway—uncover our problems? Perhaps, but not in this order. When we uncover problems as a result of reducing our buffer against the problems, we may not be able to effectively respond to them. The pressure to deal with the impact of a problem may outweigh any effective solution to the problem. We end up applying Band-Aids™ when major surgery is needed, or we install temporary work, which invariably become institutionalized procedure. In addition, we may conclude that our inventory reduction program is not working.

Once we reach this conclusion, there is tremendous temptation to build inventory back up, to sit back, and say, "I told you inventory reduction wouldn't work for us. It may be okay for some companies but we are different." This conclusion is deadly!

Can we avoid this trap? Yes. The challenge is first to improve our response systems and then reduce the inventory that depends on those systems. As we improve our response systems and gain confidence in our ability to respond, we can begin to gradually reduce the inventory, which was a buffer against our inability to respond.

When we approach inventory this way, we not only protect ourselves against the reasons why the stuff was there in the first place, but we also improve our chances for success.

Success without risk is the answer. This difference between relying on inventory to respond and developing our internal systems to make them responsive is what distinguishes the inventory-based competitor from the response-managed organization. Success without risk is important to response-managed organizations. They have made response the centerpiece of their corporate competitive strategy. They strive to provide ever improved levels of response to evolving and expanding market expectations. This is very different from the inventory-based approach to response.

Reliance on inventory as the primary vehicle for maintaining competitive customer service levels is a worst-of-all-worlds alternative. This approach drives the using organization into a state of frantic mobility in which resources are continually being diverted to respond to the crisis of the moment arising from the deficiencies of response through inventory.

This approach places very little, if any, emphasis on solving underlying causes and instead invests heavily in building more stuff. It is necessary always to produce more stuff because, no matter what we do, the mix of finished goods inventory always seems to be wrong. Companies taking this approach often find themselves operating in a purely reactive mode, always trying to catch up.

One of the difficulties with using inventory to alleviate response problems is the need to base inventory levels on forecasts, a subject on which we can be assured of consensus. *Forecasts will always be wrong!* No matter what method is used to determine the forecast, the results will be wrong. At best, a forecast is our hope of what our customers will want—*our* hope, not necessarily *their* hope. They always seem to want something different from what was forecast.

The only unknown about a forecast is how wrong will it be. Were we close or way off base this time? Of course, we always try to do better next time. This sets up a catch-22 situation. A company relies on forecasts because its response capabilities are inadequate to the needs of customers. It does not have the resources to respond in any other way. So how should it invest inadequate, scarce resources? The answer generally seems to be to produce stuff that no one will want. This further reduces the availability of resources to produce what customers really want, which causes the company to build more buffer stock, which creates other deficiencies, in a never-ending cycle of reaction. The inventory-based organization will find itself in a continual state of turmoil, as it tries to adjust to the discrepancies between hope and reality.

Once this state of reaction is reached, it becomes increasingly difficult to keep up. Quality problems grow. After all, no one has the time to slow down and deal with them. For the same reason, maintenance problems grow and further contribute to quality problems. Material shortage problems grow, employee morale sinks, productivity diminishes, the ability to respond diminishes, causing each of these situations to become more critical. This situation often results in the organization's reaching a state of equilibrium in which all departments and personnel are operating at the lowest level of capability possible and sustaining this performance level. Frustration and diminishing profits are the two primary constants defining this type of organization.

The response-managed organization has a name for this type of competitor: victim. This type of competitor is easy prey for the response-managed organization, which is able to provide superior levels of service to customers without incurring the negatives associated with inventory-based response. Response-managed organizations build on each success. Inventory-based competitors move from crisis to crisis, always reacting to events over which they have little or no control. Response-managed organizations fix causes; inventory-based competitors tend to invest in solving effects. One approach is permanent; the root cause of a problem is eliminated. The other is illusory, providing only temporary relief, at best, from the effect of the moment.

Teamwork

I will be better tomorrow than I was yesterday
because of our interaction today!
                                                STEVE LEVIT

There is no question that a management transformation is taking place within many internationally competitive companies. They are evolving from typical authoritarian management styles to more effective teamwork styles.

Numerous attributes are associated with the teamwork approach: trust, a common sense of purpose, communication, mutual respect, coaching, risk taking, and many other attributes, chief of which are trust, trust, and more trust. Trust is the foundation for establishing successful teams. Labor must completely trust management, and management must fully trust labor. Management must trust management, and labor must trust labor. Without trust, effective communication is not possible. Without communication, effective team interaction is not possible. Without effective team interaction, productive teamwork is not possible.

One of the primary elements of trust is tolerance—tolerance of others, and tolerance of the differences between each and every one of us. During my life, I have observed that:

Those seeking offense, never fail to find it.

As a society, we seem to be headed toward increasing intolerance. Our society, instead of growing more homogeneous, appears to be dividing itself into special interest groups. It seems that each day a new special interest group is formed. Each group represents a collection of people who have staked out an unswerving position on something or who find offense in some action taken by others—they.

As each new group arises, its intolerance for opponents or nonmembers grows. The more groups there are, the greater the all-around level of intolerance. Instead of celebrating diversity, we angrily denounce it while proclaiming our new vision of brotherhood—brotherhood based on the tenet that sounds something like this:

If only they could realize how what they are doing is hurting everyone. We are acting as their agents because they are unwilling to take action on their own. Therefore, they should change their [values, beliefs, convictions, etc.].

It is "their" responsibility to become brothers with "us." Those seeking to find offense seem to be driven by righteous indignation, which is nourished by a certainty that their actions represent what is "good." Others who do not agree, by definition, represent that which is not good; they are blemished individuals.

As righteous indignation grows, the need to support opinion with fact diminishes. The end becomes more than justifying the means. In fact, neither end nor means is subject to criticism or review any longer. Their offense provides motive and reason for our actions. Both ends and means become flexible, driven by the many possible offenses that those seeking offense never fail to find.

Effective teamwork requires that we transcend offense. We must seek ways to reconcile differences and to grow and prosper in spite of our diversity. Diversity is strength. From diversity comes perspectives other than our own. If we use them to our advantage, then we all benefit. If instead we seek only to find reason for offense, we also will never fail to find it. Offense will always get in the way of teamwork.

When offense exists, trust is diminished. After all, how can *we* trust those who continue to offend us. And, of course, how can *we* trust those who always seem to take offense at whatever we do. Which *we* prevails?

In its most basic form, this feeling of trust translates into management's having faith in the ability of labor to perform to a high standard of excellence without continual management involvement. It is trust that labor seeks to excel rather than to just get by. Labor must trust in management, feel secure in their jobs, and feel neither pressured to perform to unrealistic performance levels, nor subject to capricious judgment. As human beings, we are fallible. The best we can do, as a result of experience, learning, and shared responsibility, is to minimize the mistakes while we strive to excellence. Excellence is enhanced in a team environment.

When this type of trust becomes the reality, many positive results can be obtained. A good example of this is the Japanese policy of resisting layoffs, compared to the prevalent American tendency to cut labor costs at every opportunity or at the slightest sign of adversity. Let's examine the results of these two very different approaches.

In the American approach, when a company is confronted with a downturn in business or with virtually any economic adversity, one of its first actions is to "restructure," which means "lay people off." The laid-off are rarely those making the decision to lay off people. The decision makers are protected from the consequences of their prior actions. This approach creates an environment in which the immediate concern of each employee is to ensure that he or she is not among those who are "restructured." At individual manufacturing facilities, people tend to become fatalistic, awaiting the ax. Overall performance diminishes as morale diminishes and as enthusiasm for the job and towards the company diminishes. All sense of employee involvement and loyalty towards the organization is lost; individual survival replaces any feelings of mutual cooperation or teamwork.

Now let's look at the Japanese approach. In this environment employees are guaranteed job security. They are totally involved in company affairs. They feel as though they are part of a family—in which all members have a responsibility to work together to ensure the success of the family. When adversity strikes, this sense of family results in a pulling together to find ways to overcome the adversity. Instead of being concerned primarily with the individual, they become even more organizationally oriented and seek ways in which they all can contribute, in a positive way, toward overcoming the threat to the "family." *New opportunities are found. New products and markets are explored. Adversity truly becomes a stimulus for opportunity instead of being an excuse for failure.*

Which approach will provide both short-term and long-term success? You decide.

While you are reaching a decision, let's examine some of the costs associated with these two approaches, to see if how labor costs are evaluated has any impact on the types of decisions made.

In many American companies, labor is not well trained. The tendency is not to invest hard earned dollars to increase the learning and education of labor beyond the very minimum required to accomplish day-to-day tasks. After all, many manufacturing jobs are viewed as avocations, which can be filled by almost anyone with a minimum of training. Labor is not expected to have knowledge of how they contribute to or deduct from corporate profits. How we account for costs and how much profit we make is information reserved for executive levels of the organization, not something labor should be concerned about. Labor need not concern themselves with such abstractions as teamwork skills or academic quality skills, since these only serve as a distraction from the required job skills. We certainly would not want workers daydreaming about these issues while on the job.

In short, too often, the belief is that labor is an easily replenishable resource that is neither highly skilled, trained, nor indispensable. The costs associated with rehiring people, with training or retraining, with reduced performance during the training periods, with compromised product and job quality resulting from a lack of experience, with a reduction in morale—all these consequences are either ignored or dismissed when compared to the apparent savings in direct labor costs realized from a layoff. In other words, we look at the hourly price of this labor, ignoring the costs associated with its loss and/or acquisition. We also, too often, overlook labor as a value-adding resource, able to contribute beyond their immediate job requirement.

Most Japanese corporations view labor very differently. They view labor as a valuable resource that is necessary to achieve the high levels of quality and productivity required of top-performing companies. They invest in expanding the abilities of their labor force to ensure that they are capable of understanding not only their immediate jobs but also the relationship of their jobs to the overall success of the organization. They invest in increasing awareness of how departments, functions, and jobs interact, affecting each other and, in turn, being affected. They invest in ensuring that all employees are capable of participating in team efforts that are focused on improving the performance of their company. The company invests in its resources, and its resources have a vested interest in returning a profit on the investment.

The result of this approach is improvement in product and process quality, an energized and alert work force, countless employee suggestions, teamwork, cooperation, and success by any measure applied. Overall, this type of organization will realize greater customer satisfaction with their products, and will be more capable of responding quickly to ever changing market and customer demands. Profits increase, costs decrease, and stability improves dramatically. *These companies fully understand the difference between the price of labor and the cost of labor to an organization.* They understand the difference between the price of education and the cost of ignorance!

These are some reasons why companies such as Toyota or Toshiba have cash reserves of $15 billion and $10 billion instead of being highly leveraged and in debt as a result of takeovers, mergers, and acquisitions.

Which position would you prefer for your company?

Teamwork means more than groups of people meeting together. Effective teamwork requires efforts and qualities that, when missing, transform the teamwork into a mere gathering of individuals. Team environments are an improvement over individual effort environments. High-performance team environments are an improvement over ordinary team environments. The demands of response-managed competition call for high-performance teams.

Can we distinguish ordinary teams from high-performance teams? Yes. Is it important to achieve high-performance levels? Yes. No matter how capable individuals are or believe themselves to be, their abilities in a high-performance team environment will be expanded well beyond their abilities as individuals. The synergism generated in a team environment is a powerful development tool. In the response-managed team environment, teams are empowered to make decisions. Teams are not formed to produce reports, which are presented to other decision-making teams or individuals. After all, if the output of the team cannot be trusted, why was the team formed in the first place?

This does not mean that teams completely replace management in the decision cycle. It means only that management has the confidence to manage in a team environment. In this environment, teams are expected to be capable of reaching conclusions and deciding issues without being subjected to ongoing review of their actions. Management may approve team decisions, but, the approval process is more to ensure extended understanding of the decision than to review and approve the decision. *In other words, teams are formed for the specific purpose of making specific decisions.*

Teams may be composed of people from a specific department or from different departments and functions. High-performance teams exhibit observable characteristics that are specific and measurable. Some of these characteristics are:

Common sense of purpose. Team members understand and share a common sense of purpose. Purpose defines why the team was formed.

Clearly understood goals. The team understands why the team was formed and what goals are to be achieved. *Goals* are specific objectives within the general purpose for which the team was formed. They define the results the team is expected to achieve.

Empowerment to produce the results. The team should be expected to achieve the goals set for the team and be empowered to take the actions necessary to realize those goals. The team should be trusted to take responsibility for their actions. Continual management oversight of team activities is not required. Teams are empowered to rely on the resources within the team and to utilize outside resources when required.

A high level of trust and openness in communication. Team members must trust each other and be capable of communicating openly among themselves. A feeling of trust must also exist between team members and their respective management.

Genuine concern and support for one another. Team members not only trust each other but exhibit concern for each other. Team members will be more interested in supporting each other than in promoting individual performance at the expense of another team member. Each team member is considered capable of contributing to the success of the team.

Participation by everyone. Team members strive to support each other and to encourage each other to participate in team activities. Those who are more outspoken are able to show restraint and encourage the more reticent members to speak up. Those who may be reticent will be patiently encouraged to interact and participate in team activities.

A "risk-taking" environment. Teams should be willing to take chances. Teams should always question the "why" of things and be prepared to proceed down new paths. Personal risk is minimized as team members interact, support each other, and share in risk taking.

An effective system for communicating accurate data. Team members should develop or have an effective system for communicating with each other. Effective communication is a requirement during team meetings as well as between formal meetings. Any effective communication method will include steps for ensuring the accuracy of data and information being communicated.

Win/win resolutions to conflicts. When people meet to form teams, they must be prepared to encounter conflicts. The issue is not whether conflict will occur, it will; the issue is how will the conflict be resolved. A win/win approach to resolving conflict will provide greater benefits than a win/lose approach. High-performance team members are results-oriented. They recognize that the team is a more capable vehicle for reaching a quality result than any individual. Team attributes—such as mutual support, trust, empowerment, communication and so forth—all contribute to an environment in which individual effort is directed toward team achievement. Traditional I-win/you-lose approaches are counterproductive in this environment.

Planning before action. Teams plan a course of action before acting. They are able to balance between an aim-aim-aim-aim-fire approach and an aim-fire-fire-fire-fire approach. They are capable of rapidly accumulating information and of rapidly processing that information to reach viable conclusions on which to plan subsequent action.

Removal of barriers to creativity. In the high-performance team environment, barriers to creativity have been removed. There are generally many such barriers to remove, and they can vary within different situations. One of the greatest barriers to creativity is the "atta boy" syndrome: People may hold back ideas for fear of *not* getting an "atta boy." We must feel free to be wrong in order to truly be creative.

Brainstorming to generate ideas. Teams will use brainstorming as a way to generate ideas. In this approach, any and all suggestions, ideas, insights, or comments are encouraged without evaluation. Once idea collection has ceased, the accumulated suggestions can be discussed and evaluated.

A system for making high-quality decisions. The team will have developed a process for making decisions. Team members understand how they will proceed towards reaching the decisions necessary to achieve team goals. The decision path is not haphazard or random; it is deliberate and specific.

Utilization of the capabilities of all team members. The individual capabilities of team members will vary. Each team member contributes to the team in accordance with his or her individual capabilities, which are not necessarily similar or equal among team members. Membership on a high-performance team carries with it the responsibility to contribute individual knowledge and capability to the team. Shared capability aids in improving the quality of team output.

Room for different people to lead, based on the expertise needed. Teams are typically comprised of diverse capabilities and cross-functional representation. Teams need to deal with information and data from many sources and functions, and to assimilate this input to achieve specific results. The team members should be capable enough to assign leadership of team discussions to whichever team member most capably represents the topics being discussed. This approach allows each team member to best utilize and contribute individual expertise toward collective success.

Shared responsibility and accountability for meetings. As team members share leadership based on expertise, they start to assume a mutual responsibility for team actions and results. Team members should be individually, as well as collectively, accountable to each other for the success of team performance.

Perception of change as an opportunity for growth. Team members are not afraid of change, viewing it as an opportunity for growth. Team members understand that the only constant in a response-managed competitive environment is change. *Change implies steady growth and progress toward an ever evolving goal, which is defined by technology, market desires, customer requirements, and the development of new methods and standards of performance.*

Quick identification and action on opportunities. Team members are prepared to seek out and identify new opportunities, taking appropriate action as they see fit. Teams are empowered to take action.

Enjoyment of the challenge of solving difficult problems. Team members are problem solvers. They are not afraid of confronting difficult situations, and they are confident of their abilities to respond appropriately. Virtually all prior team attributes contribute toward an environment in which effective problem solving can flourish.

Continuous search for new ways to improve. High-performance team members are not satisfied with the status quo. They continually seek new ways to perform old tasks and to replace old tasks. They understand that excellence is a momentary event that is always undergoing challenges by new ways of performing traditional tasks. Only change is permanent. Everything else is fleeting.

Teams that exhibit these characteristics are capable of achieving excellent results quickly and consistently. The business environment that is capable of sustaining these types of teams will be able to rapidly adapt to whatever circumstances fate and the markets dictate.

Productivity and Stuff

If you wanted it yesterday, why didn't you wait until tomorrow to ask?

Too often we get productivity and "stuff" confused. We tend to equate the creation of stuff with productivity. We believe that, the more stuff we create, the more productive we are. This traditional approach has served as our measure of productivity for almost as long as man has been manufacturing stuff. Is this, then, a truth that is self-evident and is to be revered throughout time?

Modern manufacturing practices would seem to indicate otherwise. Production of lots of stuff means nothing more than that we have produced lots of stuff. If it is the right stuff, we were productive. If it is the wrong stuff, not only is it not productive; it is unprofitable.

What is the "right stuff"? What is the "wrong stuff"? The right stuff is what our customers want, need, and will pay us for if we can provide it to them. Anything else is the wrong stuff. Let's be clear about this: If what we are producing is not immediately going out the door to a customer, it is wrong. Investing our assets to produce the wrong stuff reduces profits, reduces productivity, reduces customer satisfaction, reduces efficiency, and increases inventory. This is not good stuff. Investing resources to produce the wrong stuff, in the form of either goods or services, inhibits our overall ability to respond effectively to customer needs. In this sense, "stuff" can be a response inhibitor.

Is having stuff really all that bad? Is it so diametrically opposed to productivity? After all, eventually this stuff may go to customers. This line of argument leads us to the issue of productivity or profit. Can an organization have both? Or must it sacrifice one to attain the other? The answers are discussed in the next chapter.

7

Rethinking the Present... Discovering the Future (Part I)

Reengineering ... adding value ... stockpiling inventory ... building in quality. Is there any one solution to the problem of putting an organization on an equal footing with global competitors? The solutions are many, and they may be had by rethinking what we are now doing, how we are doing it, and why we think we are doing things right.

In this chapter we will examine current thinking on the issues of setting goals, accounting, adding value, and bring new products to the marketplace.

In the next chapter, we will follow up with discussions of quality, the lessons we can learn from our overseas competitors, and the role of technology.

Bull's-Eye? Setting Goals

"I shot an arrow in the air, it fell to ground I know not where." This approach describes the decision process traditionally employed in most of American industry today. Restating the situation, I instituted a program designed to improve my operational performance only to find that the situation did not improve.

Gaining insight into why and how this can happen is a critical first step in defining your future. How can so many well intentioned executives, instituting so many well intentioned programs, achieve so little in the way of positive results?

This is not to imply that all attempts yield marginal results. Indeed, some companies have achieved dramatic sustainable positive results. We all recognize those who have and who are adopting sustainable programs, organizations such as: HP, Wal-Mart, Motorola, Honda (U.S. Operations), Xerox, as well as those who have not fared as well: General Motors, Chrysler, Sears, and IBM. The key word in all the success stories is *sustainable*. This is the defining characteristic. If the benefit is only short-term, we soon have to catch up to a new unanticipated competitive challenge. Instead, the benefit has to be long-term and capable of providing support to the next level of attainment necessary to ensure competitive leadership.

The difference between fleeting and lasting benefits is one of definition—how the organization defines the bullseye. Let's look at two examples to illustrate this difference: first the setting of objectives, and second the result of establishing these objectives.

"Have you ever been involved in a cost-cutting program of one sort or another?" When this question is asked of audiences, invariably the answer is, "Of course, we have"—accompanied by a strange look of wonderment at such an obvious question. The next question is, "Why? Why did your organization institute a cost-cutting program?" The answer to this question is also uniformly similar: "To improve profits." The next question—"Did it work?"—gets varying answers: "No." "Only for a short time. Then the problems created by the cuts began to kill us." Very rarely is this last question answered with an unqualified yes.

What went wrong? Surely the intention to increase profits is desirable. How can one fault a desire to reduce costs? The difference lies in the fact that these two intentions—raising profits and lowering costs—often get confused. The tendency is to believe that they are causally related.

But let's see if the cost-cutting bull's-eye wins the profit improvement prize.

Defining the Bull's-Eye Affects How We Aim

When we define the bull's-eye as cutting costs, the steps we take to hit this target will be actions that cut costs. Cost-cutting actions are usually very different from the steps we would take if the bull's-eye were improving profits.

Not only does each definition carry its own related actions, each is very different in its implication: Cutting cost is negative, implying that something will be removed from our operations—things that incur costs. Improving profit is positive, implying that something will be added to the organization—more profit.

These distinctions affect all the decisions subsequently made in the hope of hitting the target. When we embark on a cost-cutting program, we view decisions by that parameter: "Will the result of this decision be a reduction in the cost of something? Rarely, if at all, is the decision considered on the basis of its impact on profit. After all, profit is not the stated objective; cost reduction is!

When the real objective, profit, becomes the parameter for evaluating decisions, we will reach very different decisions and achieve very different results. A profit improvement approach is more likely to actually improve profits than will a cost-cutting approach. In the profit improvement mode, cost is allocated in a manner appropriate to improving profit. Cost, or investment, may even increase when improving profit is the bull's-eye.

Which bull's-eye has the better chance of achieving a positive, sustainable result? Profit improvement is the hands-down winner.

Let's examine some possible decisions and the result of these decisions using the parameters of cost and profit. For our example, consider two hypothetical companies. Each is in electronics, although they are not identical in size, and they do not make the same product. While these companies are hypothetical, they are composites based on real organizations.

Company A. The organization is facing many competitive challenges. Revenues are decreasing, market share is eroding, and foreign competition is winning business from many of their prime customers.

They are confronted with numerous problems, product quality is poor, and reject rates are in excess of 20 percent.

Customer service is not responsive. Quotes can take from days to months depending on complexity and on how much custom design is required. Costs are rising, while competitive price pressure is driving down prices and margins.

Their future does not look bright.

Company B. This firm is an industry leader in their product line. Their products are stable and provide exceptional profit margins. Cash rich, they are investing in technology to maintain market dominance. Customer service levels are good. They will ship products on the same or next day following an order. This level of service is maintained by utilizing extensive finished goods inventories. Stockouts occur no more than 15 percent of the time.

They are confronted with some problems. Improvement programs of all sorts typically produce marginal or no results. They rely on new technology to keep pace in the market place, and this technology helps them to cut costs and thereby maintain their high margins. They do not consider the cost of inventory when evaluating customer service levels. Quality is an issue, but they can afford to absorb a high percent of rejected products because of their very high profit margins.

Management is traditional. There is very little interaction between management and labor at any level of the organization. Functions are rigidly compartmented.

Company A will adopt a profit improvement approach to addressing their problems. Company B will adopt a more traditional cost-cutting approach.

Company B.   Using a traditional approach, they place primary emphasis on reducing direct labor costs. To this end they initiate several studies: One is directed at exploring the acquisition of new equipment that can reduce direct labor costs; another looks at the advantages of moving manufacturing operations to Mexico. At the same time, they are looking to Engineering to find new lower-cost materials for products and for ways to introduce automation to reduce labor costs. Marketing accepts cutbacks in production providing inventory levels are first built up to ensure customer demand coverage. Engineering and QC agree to develop a comprehensive quality management approach for manufacturing to reduce product reject rates. The quality improvement program is introduced to shop floor personnel, who will be required to utilize it to reduce defects.

Maintenance personnel are reduced in an attempt to reduce costs. Maintenance stores are also reduced in an effort to cut inventory costs without sacrificing customer service levels.

Labor will be asked to share in the cost reduction effort by freezing pay levels for an undetermined period of time. Management bonuses, however, remain intact as a reward for the bold steps they are initiating to improve their competitive position.

They attempt to retain or increase market share by offering high-quality, low-cost products to their customers. They cut costs so that they can retain their high margin objectives. They drop several products from their product line that are no longer capable of providing the high margins they desire.

Company A. Starting from a position of weakness, they do not have the resources to invest in capital projects to reduce labor costs; they have to make do with what they have and try to prosper. Instead of seeking ways to cut costs, they develop a strategy designed to improve profits. This strategy is focused on increasing market share and profit for the products produced and sold. They focus on improving their response systems. They plan to take their competition by surprise by initiating a quick strike intended to penetrate new markets and to increase market share by offering potential customers real business inducements to do business with them. As a result of their profit improvement efforts, they come to realize that they too are, in fact, customers to their suppliers and that, as customers, they require certain attributes from their suppliers if they are to improve their profitability.

Company A

Emphasis: Improving profits.

Objective: Proactive, aimed at increasing market share, improving ability of the organization to respond to customers, and taking competition by surprise.

Actions: To better understand their business needs and also the business needs of their customers.

To reengineer all internal systems, making them more responsive to market and customer needs.

To improve manufacturing operation, reducing manufacturing cycle times and lot sizes.

To introduce new better-designed products, expanding their product offerings to customers.

Approach: Innovative, external focus on better understanding needs of customers and marketing directly to those needs.

Internal changes will be driven by requirements of customers and focused on improving their ability to respond to customers.

Competitive strategy is to be the high-value provider to their customers; they will end up charging more for their products.

Investment: In education and training programs; in research to better understand needs of customers.

Unable to support major capital investment projects. Will invest in ways to better use existing resources and facilities.

Company B

Emphasis: Reducing direct labor costs.

Objective: Reactive, aimed at allowing them to maintain the status quo in the market place.

Actions: To initiate studies: feasibility of move to Mexico; use of new equipment, each aimed at reducing direct labor costs.

To increase finished goods inventory in order to be able to reduce direct labor resources; to reduce scrap and rework by instituting a quality program for production.

To find lower-cost materials, to cut production and maintenance personnel.

To freeze labor pay rates.

To drop less profitable products from product line.

Approach: Traditional internal focus. Benefits will result by reducing internal costs. Approach to market place is that of commodity provider.

Customer response capabilities based on inventory position.

Competitive strategy is primarily offering low-cost products.

Investment: In studies to find ways to reduce direct labor costs and material costs.

Willing to undertake major capital spending to achieve cost reduction objectives (almost seems like an oxymoron!)—new capital equipment, cost of moving to Mexico, consulting costs in support of these objectives.

Projected results: They will most likely achieve their objectives to increase market share and profit.

The steps initiated will expand their product offerings, provide them with a stronger marketing approach than that used by their competition.

They will leverage their improved manufacturing capabilities to reduce operating overhead, eventually allowing them to reduce product pricing while maintaining higher profit margins than their competitors'.

They will enjoy continued growth corresponding to their ability to realize additional saving from increasing production quantities.

They will charge more for their products, but it will cost their customers less to do business with them.

The internal changes they are making to become responsive will have a long-term impact on their organization. They will be much more flexible than when they started out. As a result, they will be better positioned to adapt to ever changing market demands, in most instances, without incurring major expenditures.

They will take advantage of their improved product design abilities and lead their competition in introducing new and innovative products.

Their customer base will continue to grow as they take business from their competitors.

Their profits will grow as their margins and market share increase.

Projected results: They will also achieve their objective of reducing costs.

They will, however, probably continue to experience a shrinking customer base.

They will lose customers and market share to company A.

They will continue to lose customers as a result of their shrinking product line.

They will further reduce their product line when margins drop.

They will lose flexibility in responding to future changes in product lines as a result of their investment in automation. The new equipment they will acquire will be associated with existing products and processes.

Emerging market demand for new products will require new equipment and methods. They will be trapped by their now old/new equipment in which they have to justify their sunk costs.

Problems associated with Mexican customs and production will require an increase in finished goods inventory to maintain position in remaining markets.

This requirement was not evaluated during their initial investigation of Mexico, which focused primarily on the difference in labor rates.

Profit margins will likely diminish as they strive to maintain market share by cutting costs.

With this realization they are confronted by a BFO—blinding flash of the obvious. Their customers would probably desire the same attributes they would like from their suppliers. What if they were to actively offer the same attributes to their customers? Wouldn't this approach allow their customers to realize the same advantages that they were seeking from their suppliers? What impact would this approach have on their competition if they, the competition, were competing on the basis of product cost, not value added?

They enlarge on this BFO concept by wondering what would happen if they could also expand their product line to become more of a full-service provider. They find their strategy. Without realizing it they decide to become response-managed organizations. They will compete on the basis not of product cost, but of value-added for their customers. They have a pretty good understanding of these values based on their own needs.

Having agreed on this strategy, they begin to make the changes to the organization necessary for them to be capable of delivering on their promise of response. They begin to reengineer their internal systems to eliminate nonproductive, time-consuming activities. To their delight, they find that they could accomplish most of these objectives without incurring much capital investment. They do not have to acquire new resources. They find ways to use existing resources better.

This applies to all their resources, human and machine alike. They develop manufacturing methods that allow them to reduce production lot sizes. They also reduce manufacturing cycle time, improve order processing time, decrease their new product engineering development cycle time, and begin to design products for manufacturability.

They quietly develop a marketing strategy aimed at capturing market share from company B and at developing new business opportunities. They select several of company B's largest customers as targets.

Without dwelling on why each company chose a particular approach, which one do you think will be successful? Company A has the better chance of prevailing. They will win and win big. Company B is positioning themselves for a big loss.

Let's evaluate the steps proposed by each company. Each company should meet their objectives. However, I propose that company B will not be able to compete with company A, and will eventually lose their position as industry leader.

The profiles of each company are admittedly contrived, but they accurately reflect real-life situations. I have had experience with more than one of each type of company.

As response-managed organizations, we must be careful to ensure that we know our target. We cannot afford to invest time and resources striving to hit the wrong bull's-eye.

The Accounting Trap

What happens when people with good intentions take actions intended to provide benefit and advantage, but instead diminish and detract from the intended benefits? They have fallen victim to "the accounting trap."

There is a wonderful story entitled, "Through the Jungle of Accounting Logic with Gun and Camera." This story eloquently describes what can happen when accounting practices lose sight of the environment in which they are being applied and of the results to be attained.* It illustrates "the accounting trap."

A Tragedy In One Act

THE SCENE: A small store deep in the jungle of accounting.

THE TIME: Today—and tomorrow, if you aren't careful.

THE CAST: An unknown Profit Analysis Expert, and Joe, Owner and Operator of a small store-restaurant in the jungle.

As the curtain rises, we find Joe dusting his counter and casting admiring glances at a shiny new rack holding brightly colored bags of peanuts. The rack sits at the end of the counter. The store itself is like all small store-restaurants in the jungle of accounting logic. It is a clean, well lighted joint, patronized by the neighborhood residents and an occasional juvenile delinquent. As Joe dusts and admires his new peanut rack, he listens almost uncomprehendingly, to the earnest speeches of the Profit Analysis Expert.

PA: Joe, you said you put in these peanuts because some people ask for them, but do you realize what this rack of peanuts is *costing* you?

---

*I was given a copy of this story by a friend who received it from a friend. I do not know when, where, or by whom this story was created.

JOE: It ain't gonna cost. 'S gonna be a profit. Sure, I hadda pay $25 for a fancy rack to holda bags, but the peanuts cost 6 cents a bag and I sell 'em for 10 cents. Figger I sell 50 bags a week to start. It'll take 12 or so weeks to cover the cost of the rack. After that I gotta clear profit of 4 cents a bag. The more I sell, the more I make.

PA: That is an antiquated and completely unrealistic approach, Joe. Fortunately, modern accounting procedures permit a more accurate picture, which reveals the complexities involved.

JOE: Huh?

PA: To be precise, those peanuts must be integrated into your entire operation and be allocated their appropriate share of business overhead. They must share a proportionate part of your expenditures for rent, heat, light, equipment depreciation, decorating, salaries for your waitresses, cook ...

JOE: The cook? Whut's he gotta do wit' peanuts?

PA: Look, Joe, the cook is in the kitchen, the kitchen prepares the food, the food is what brings people in, and, while they're in, they ask to buy peanuts. That's why you must charge a portion of the cook's wages, as well as a part of your own salary to peanut sales. This sheet contains a carefully calculated cost analysis, which indicates the peanut operation should pay exactly $1278 per year toward these general overhead costs.

JOE: The peanuts? $1278 a year for overhead? That's nuts!

PA: It's really a little more than that. You also spend money each week to have the window washed, to have the place swept out in the morning, keep soap in the washroom, and provide free cokes to the police. That raises the total to $1313 per year.

JOE: [Thoughtfully] But the peanut salesman said I'd make money. Put 'em to the end of the counter, he said, and get 4 cents a bag profit.

PA: [With a sniff] He's not an accountant. Do you actually know what the portion of the counter occupied by the peanut rack is worth to you?

JOE: Ain't worth nothing—no stool there—just a dead spot at the end.

PA: The modern cost picture permits no dead spots. Your counter contains 60 square feet, and your counter business grosses $15,000 a year. Consequently, the square foot of space occupied by the peanut rack is worth $250 per year. Since you have taken that area away from general counter use, you must charge the value of the space to the occupant.

JOE: You mean I gotta add *$250 a year more* to the *peanuts?*

PA: Right. That raises their share of the general operating costs to a grand total of $1563 per year. Now then, if you sell 50 bags of peanuts per week, these allocated costs will amount to 60 cents per bag.

JOE: [Incredulously] *What?*

PA: Obviously, to that must be added your purchase price of 6 cents per bag, which brings the total to 66 cents. So you see, by selling peanuts at 10 cents per bag you are losing 56 cents on every sale.

JOE: Somethin's crazy!

PA: Not at all! Here are the *figures*. They *prove* your peanut operation cannot stand on its own feet.

JOE: [Brightening] Suppose I sell lotsa peanuts—a thousand bags a week. Would that help?

PA: [Tolerantly] Joe, you don't understand the problem. If the volume of peanut sales increases, your operating costs will go up. You'll have to handle more bags, with more time, more general overhead, more everything. The basic principle of accounting is firm on that subject: "The bigger the operation the more general overhead costs that must be allocated." No. Increasing the volume of sales won't help.

JOE: Okay. You're so smart. *You* tell *me* what I gotta do.

PA: [Condescendingly] Well—you could first reduce operating expenses.

JOE: How?

PA: Take smaller space in an older building with cheaper rent. Cut salaries. Wash the windows biweekly. Have the floor swept only on Thursday. Remove the soap from the washrooms. Cut out the cokes for the cops. This will also help you decrease the square foot value of your counter. For example, if you can cut your expenses 50 percent that will reduce the amount allocated to peanuts from $1563 down to $781.50 per year, reducing the cost to 36 cents per bag.

JOE: [Slowly] That's better?

PA: Much, much better. However, even then you would lose 26 cents per bag if you charge only 10 cents. Therefore, you must also raise your selling price. If you want a net profit of 4 cents per bag, you would have to charge 40 cents.

JOE: [Flabbergasted] You mean even after I cut operating costs 50 percent, I still gotta charge 40 cents for a 10-cent bag of peanuts? Nobody's that nuts about nuts! Who'd buy 'em.

PA: That's a secondary consideration. The point is that, at 40 cents, you'd be selling at a price based upon a true and proper evaluation of your then reduced costs.

JOE: [Eagerly] Look! I gotta better idea. Why don't I just throw the nuts out—put 'em in the ash can?

PA: Can you afford it?

JOE: Sure, all I got is about 50 bags of peanuts—about three bucks. So I lose $25 on the rack, but I'm outa this nutsy business and no more grief.

PA: [Shaking head] Joe, it isn't quite that simple. You are in the peanut business! The minute you throw these peanuts out you are adding $1563 of annual overhead to the *rest* of your operation. Joe—be realistic—*can you afford to do that?*

JOE: [Completely crushed] It's unbelievable! Last week I was makin' money. Now I'm in trouble, just because I think peanuts on a counter is gonna bring me some extra profit, just because I believe 50 bags of peanuts a week is easy.

PA: [With raised eyebrow] That is the reason for modern cost studies, Joe—to dispel those false illusions.

Joe just fell victim to "the accounting trap."

How does the accounting trap apply to manufacturing? Why is there apparent conflict between productivity and profit? How do we arrive at this disturbing dilemma?

In manufacturing organizations, the calculation of product cost and profit margin are of critical importance to the success and endurance of the organization. On the surface, these calculations appear to be straightforward and simple, providing results that all agree to and that benefit the organization. When we calculate product cost, there is not much involved. We only have to deal with three issues: material costs, labor costs, and overhead application. Once we know our costs, we can determine our selling price. If this is a larger number than our costs, we have made a profit. There is hardly any room to go wrong. We should be able to make viable business decisions based on the outcome of our financial analysis.

Why then, do we go astray? The simple answer is that the assumptions underlying how we calculate labor contribution and overhead are not conducive to establishing a product cost that is related to actual manufacturing events or costs. Nor are they conducive to supporting certain business decisions. Some of these assumptions are:

Efficiency can be measured by comparing actual production numbers to the established standards at a manufacturing operation. If the production numbers are equal to or greater than the standard, then we are efficient.

Capacity is a function of efficiency. The standards established for each machine or operation determine the manufacturing capacity of our operations.

Productivity means performing to standard and fully utilizing the available capacity of a manufacturing operation.

Capital investment should be dispersed over as many items as possible. The more parts we can run through an operation, the lower the cost per part.

Cost cutting will increase profits.

Direct labor is an easily replenishable resource. During economically difficult times, reducing labor pools is a quick and easy way to reduce payables. After all, we can easily replace this resource; there are lots of people looking for jobs.

In the response-managed world, each of these assumptions is a response inhibitor. Each assumption, if acted on, diminishes the ability of the adopting organization to be responsive to their own needs and to customer needs. The effect of these assumptions is to divert resources from customer-coupled activities to customer-indirect activities. Let's examine the assumption that direct labor is an easily replenishable resource, as an example of how the result of this action may be very different from its intent.

There is no doubt that laying off direct labor personnel will immediately reduce the payable burdens associated with that labor group. The question is, "What is actual magnitude of savings resulting from this action?" My experience indicates that, in general, direct labor accounts for about 7 percent of product cost. Our reduction in direct labor will thus result in a lowering by this overall percentage, based on the percent of the overall labor force laid off. For our immediate purpose let's say our layoff affected 30 percent of the direct labor workforce. We could reasonably expect to have reduced our direct labor percentage by 30 percent, and the related part of the product cost would be 4.9 percent.

Maybe not—and surely not if we have not reduced the labor content required to make the product or provide the service. If the labor content remains constant, then labor costs may even go up if overtime or additional shifts are required to meet production requirements.

What indirect cost impacts could we reasonably expect as a result of the layoff? Here are some.

Impact on Trust. Trust is the foundation on which *all* advances in manufacturing or service-based operations are erected. Without trust we cannot have effective communication, teamwork, quality programs, empowerment, or performance. If the organization is to prosper, each individual must trust the motives of others in the organization. When trust breaks down, it is replaced by suspicion and distrust. People begin looking over their shoulders, and performance suffers as personal survival becomes the prevailing motivation.

There is no greater breach of trust than for management to use reductions in force as the primary means to cut costs. Trust in employment security represents a fundamental obligation between members of an organization, and it extends from the good times through the bad times. Every employee must be willing to contribute toward the attainment and longevity of good times, and be ready to accept the burdens imposed during bad times.

The organization that is not able to perform in this manner may survive in the short term but will not be able to compete over the long term. A response-managed organization will be very aware of the importance of trust. The competitive organization will realize that they cannot afford to pay the price to achieve the relatively small gains resulting from the typical reduction-in-force (RIF) approach to cost control.

Increased Overtime. This may result if the labor content required to produce the product or service does not change. We could experience an imbalance between available labor hours and demand requirements for which the only solution is overtime or added shifts. In either case, what impact will this have on cost savings?

Additional Burden to Remaining Employees. Those still in place have to take up many tasks formerly performed by those who have been laid off. What impact will this have on overall productivity, efficiency, cost, quality, and so on?

Lowered Morale.   What impact will a layoff have on the morale of remaining employees? Will they be glad that they were not laid off and content in the belief that their future remains secure? Will they instead feel insecure and uncertain about their future? If so, what impact will this have on overall performance?

The answer is that, with the strong bonds of trust broken, morale is greatly diminished.

Impeded Organizational Ability to Adopt New Methods or Technologies.   Will labor be eager to adopt new programs and technologies? Or will they be reluctant to adopt anything that they perceive as a potential threat to their job security? What impact could this type of attitude have on an organization?

Diminished Quality.   Will the uncertainty and doubt about the future, combined with a reluctance to adopt new methods and techniques, have any impact on the quality of work and product? Will increasing work hours to make up for the reduced labor force affect quality?

Decreased Productivity.   Will the remaining labor force be able to maintain levels of productivity equal to the prior staffing levels? Will changes have to be made in team, cell, or line groups to adjust for the reduction in staffing? What impact will this have on the areas affected? My experience indicates that this type of production is most effective when the teams comprising a cell, line, or other unit remains constant. Balanced teams develop their own production rhythm, which is interrupted when new people are introduced into the group.

Confused Teamwork.   Will the idea of team be compromised as personnel are reduced? Will teams become more homogenized? And what impact will this have on performance? Since trust is a major component of achieving high levels of team performance, what impact will the loss of trust have on performance?

Retarded Responsiveness.   As the ability to effectively communicate is diminished, teamwork productivity is reduced, morale is dampened, and so on, the organization becomes increasingly less able to respond effectively to competitive challenges.

Lowered Maintenance. Maintenance personnel are frequently the targets of cost-cutting programs, but rarely is the impact of reduced maintenance considered. After all, maintenance only impacts productivity, quality, capacity and materials planning, staffing decisions, inventory levels, customer delivery performance, and other areas of activity. This is hardly enough to be concerned about when compared to the savings resulting from laying off qualified maintenance personnel. After all, maintenance people are a dime a dozen! We never have any difficulty finding qualified maintenance personnel.

Retraining Costs. What about the cost associated with training replacement employees when hiring opens up again? What about the cost associated with hiring replacement employees?

Unstable Workforce, Hiring and Firing to Meet Seasonal Fluctuation. When RIF is accepted as a viable approach to managing cost, fluctuations in workforce levels will invariably occur. The magnitude of these fluctuations is affected by many issues, among which is seasonality. No surprise, then, when companies who have adopted this approach complain that they have ongoing problems with sustaining quality performance, productivity, excessive maintenance problems, erratic efficiencies, and a reliance on excessive inventories as a way to maintain acceptable customer service levels.

Ironically, these problems, are not associated with cost cutting programs. Instead they are considered the "cost of doing business."

The cost of these "indirect" impacts on organizational performance will, in most instances, far outweigh the relatively slight returns from a layoff policy. None of these impacts is inconsequential. Each can and usually will result in major cost increases and in equally great profit losses. The impact areas all affect the ability of an organization to remain competitive, to retain market share, and to respond to changing competitive demands.

Typically, a response-managed organization has crossed the Rubicon between cost and price. The response-managed decision process will evaluate this difference and act accordingly. The benefits of low price are invariably less than the corresponding cost burden that must be paid to receive them.

Other chapters address these issues in greater detail.

Anyone Can Produce a Product

Anyone can produce or sell a product. Not everyone can offer value with that product. This is a critical distinction in today's competitive arena. More and more, companies will have to decide on their competitive strategy: cost or value. Either is a valid choice. However, the choices are very different in their impact on the organization and in the security they provide within a market place.

If the choice is to compete in the market place on the basis of product or service price, then the level of competition is very clearly defined: the low-cost provider wins (a very basic principle). In this competitive arena, there are no special needs, no extra added services, no sense of urgency. There is only a desire to offer the lowest-cost product or service. This approach is most effective with buyers who place the primary emphasis on the price of purchased goods or services without regard to the cost of those goods or services.

These buyers are diminishing in number among emerging competitively progressive organizations. Customer loyalty, in the cost-at-all-cost market, extends only to the next discount offered for similar products or services. Whoever offers the "best" price gets the order. But what about brand loyalty? That too extends just as far as the next discount. Vendors choosing this approach as their competitive strategy find themselves hoping that their competition makes the same choice. They are often suprised when their competition selects the other choice, competing on the basis of value.

Those choosing the cost approach may find themselves losing premium business to competitors while retaining the low-margin business. They have reduced their competitiveness and their products or services to a "commodity" level. They are increasingly vulnerable to any competitor who can offer a lower price.

Which competitors are stealing our premium business? How are they doing it? This is no secret. Those competitors are companies that have made a deliberate choice to become response-managed organizations. They have focused all their resources on the customer and on their ability to respond to the needs of that customer. These companies well understand the difference between competing as a commodity and competing in a value-added market.

RMOs recognize the importance of response to those select buyers who also value response and who are willing to pay a premium to anyone who can provide it. They recognize that these customers prefer to buy not only the premium items, but also more of the less urgent items from the same supplier instead of from multiple suppliers.

The RMOs understand that, if they can serve their demanding customers, they can earn their business, their loyalty, and increased margins for increased service. Customers who value urgency, speed, quality, responsiveness, and cooperation will be loyal to suppliers who are capable of providing these qualities. These customers are reluctant to walk away from such a relationship. These customers, who feel a sense of urgency and who in turn wish to be responsive to their customers are willing to pay extra for that kind of capability in vendors.

The RMO deals with all aspects of business differently from traditional competitors. They purchase differently, offer value and services to their customers differently, and perform virtually all internal functions differently. The RMO also enjoys different benefits from the commodity-oriented competitor. These differences are examined in detail throughout this book.

We're Doing a Good Job, Aren't We?—Lowering the Price of Purchased Goods

In many organizations, the purchasing charter is to reduce the cost of purchased goods. Success at achieving this goal is measured by reviewing the numbers at the lower right-hand corner of purchase orders—the cost of goods. This approach tends to be straightforward in application and immune from the positive affects of technologies, such as EDI, or the adoption of world-class methods elsewhere in an organization. Such methods and technologies may not be adopted because they represent costs whose affects are not readily seen at the lower right-hand corner of the PO. Methods that lower the costs of goods or services may be seen as costs, not as benefits.

The RMO takes a different approach. The RMO understands the difference between the price of purchased goods and the cost of those goods to the organization. This buyer understands that the price may be attractive but that the cost may be too high a price to pay; the price of purchased goods ranks number six or seven on the priority list. Based on the industry in question, at least five or six other conditions are more important than the price of materials. The chances are that, if we are not satisfying these conditions, any price advantage we think has been realized is not enough to offset the real cost of that purchase to the organization.

A number of underlying assumptions support the statement that the cost is too high a price to pay. First, the stuff is being purchased for a reason. It is really needed to support a production schedule, to assist R&D efforts, to enhance employee education and training, to support maintenance, and so forth. Any of these reasons is important to an RMO.

Let's take production scheduling as an example to examine the difference between price and cost considerations. What kind of activity goes with a production schedule? We might have done material planning to support the schedule, which was developed in support of capacity planning efforts. Customers might expect delivery based on the schedule. A preventative maintenance or a staffing requirement might be based on the schedule. And we most likely developed the production schedule in response to an indication of demand or need for the product. These are only some of the areas involved and impacted by the production schedule.

- One assumption is that it is costly to change the production schedule. Frequent changes are also very detrimental to quality, productivity, and sustained customer service levels. Whenever possible, we want to avoid this type of change. Most of us realize that efficiencies are reduced when we change the production schedule.

- Assumption number two is that, because we are aware that these areas can be affected by the availability of purchased goods, we buffer ourselves against possible outages by keeping lots of inventory around, just in case something goes wrong with the vendor. Yet, even though we carry lots of raw material inventory, the mix never seems to be quite right. Too often we find ourselves in a stock-out situation of some vital component. This is not so bad. We can usually expedite the material in from the supplier. Anyway, expediting is free, isn't it, especially when we do not include expediting costs in the cost of purchased goods?

- Let's turn to assumption number three. When the price of purchased goods is the purchasing criterion, the impact of purchased goods on the rest of the organization is not considered in making a buying decision. The lower right-hand corner reigns supreme.

We can make other assumptions, but these will serve for our analysis. In our example, the supplier is giving us a great price; we can save a few cents per item against fair market price on every item we buy. *The price of the purchased goods is low.* However, the material is supposed to be here on Monday, and it does not arrive until the following week on Thursday. How are we doing? Perhaps not so well. When the buyer cannot rely on the delivery date of purchased goods, Production cannot reliably develop schedules.

The alternative is to carry extra inventory of the material as a buffer. The extra inventory is free, isn't it? With this spare cash lying around, the materials did not cost anything to acquire. It carries no cost to maintain. What else would we have done with that space anyway? We also don't like to schedule production too far in advance: It gives everybody too much time to prepare for it. It's much better to schedule production on a "hurry-up-we-need-it-now" basis. That way we don't have to pay so much attention to things like quality and preventative maintenance.

Price without reliable delivery schedules is too high a cost to pay.

What if a supplier is giving us a fair price and delivers on time as well? How are we doing then?

The stuff we ordered is here on time, all the time. We remove it from the truck, check what was received, and find that we ordered 100 widgets and our supplier shipped us 85. This has the same impact as not receiving the material on time. We can also take the same "just-in-case" steps—increase inventory and so on—as a buffer.

Price without reliable supply of material is too high a cost to pay.

Suppose the supplier is giving us a fair price, delivers on time, and ships the quantity ordered, all the time? How are we doing? The stuff we ordered is here on time and in the right quantity. We offload the truck and run the stuff through incoming inspection. We find that 15 percent of the material is out of specification and cannot be used. Déjà vu.

Price without 100-percent good quality material is too high a cost to pay.

We get the suppplier to give us a fair price, to deliver on time, to ship the quantity ordered, and to provide 100-percent quality stuff, all the time. Now how are we doing? The stuff is here on time, the quantity is right, and the quality is 100 percent good. We joyfully offload the truck—only to find that the material shipped was not the stuff we ordered. We cannot use it.

Price without delivery of the right material is too high a cost to pay.

Our supplier is giving us a fair price, delivers on time, ships the quantity ordered, provides 100-percent quality stuff, and ships the right stuff, all the time. How are we doing? The stuff is here in time, the right quantity, 100-percent good quality, and the right stuff. We offload the truck, run the material through incoming inspection, then repackage the material to fit our production requirements.

(For example, we are repackaging ICs for use in automatic insertion machines.) In handling the material during the repackaging process, some percentage is damaged.

This has the same effect as receiving the wrong quantity or wrong product, or as not receiving the product on time, or as finding that some of the product is not up to spec. We can, of course, take the same steps as always—increase inventory.

Price without having the material prepackaged to suit our manufacturing process may be too high a cost to pay.

If our supplier is trying to provide all of the services just described, we are doing well. If the supplier is not willing to work towards resolving any problems that arise in the relationship, then we're not doing so well.

Price without having a supplier who is willing to work together with us to resolve problems in the relationship is too high a cost to pay for the stuff provided by that supplier.

How are we doing in general? Now we are doing extremely well. If all we received is a low price, then we are most likely not doing well at all.

On the other hand, suppose our supplier:

- Can deliver on time all the time.
- Can deliver the right quantity all the time.
- Can deliver 100-percent quality all the time.
- Can deliver the right product all the time.
- Can prepackage the product to match our manufacturing process.
- Is willing to work together with us to resolve any problems in our relationship.
- Is charging a fair price for their products.

Should we expect still other attributes from suppliers who are codependent business partners? You bet we should.

- Our codependent suppliers should be assisting us in staying abreast of the new technologies, methods, processes, and materials that they are involved with and that may be of benefit to us, their customer, or to another customer in the chain who is affected by what we do.
- They should participate in new product design activities to ensure that we are taking advantage of their capabilities to supply quality materials.
- They should be partnering with us, perhaps making joint visits to our customers, to assist in ensuring that they understand not only our needs but the needs of our customers that are affected by their actions.
- They can be exploring new ways to communicate—ways that could reduce administrative costs and delays, or new ways to achieve payment. Perhaps immediate payment for goods can result in realizing greater discounts than are available from a net 10-, 30-, or 60-payment schedule.

You can add other attributes that pertain to your own situation.

Usually, and sadly, none of these attributes are taken into account in a purchase price reducing environment.

It Took So Long to Design That It's Obsolete: The Engineering Cycle

Traditional approaches to design engineering are based on a series of events that typically look like this:

- We conduct a marketing survey to determine the potential market for a product. This survey can take days, weeks, or months.
- Once the survey is finished, the collected information has to be collated, digested, analyzed, and finally organized into a format that supports the next required decisions. These tasks can take weeks or months.

- The organized survey information is now reviewed by the marketing group, who develop product recommendations to be presented to management and to the engineering group. This step can take weeks to months.

- The marketing recommendations are presented to management for approval and then to engineering for feasibility analysis. This step can take days to weeks.

- Engineering develops a feasibility analysis for the approved recommendations and presents their analysis to Marketing and to management. Development of this analysis can require weeks, months, or even years to complete.

- Marketing, management, and Engineering meet to review the initial recommendations in light of the feasibility studies. Together they determine which products will now be developed. This determination can be made with only a few days required for review and decision.

- Design engineering now begins the design phase for the selected products. The design phase can take ...

- Once a product is developed, it can take one of two paths: It can be shown to selected customers for approval, or it can be introduced to Manufacturing.

- Manufacturing now gears up to make the product. Equipment, manpower, materials, tooling, and other resources all have to be acquired and organized. We begin producing the product and also introduce it to the sales force.

- The sales force begins to present the product to customers.

By this time, years have passed between the initial market survey and the actual introduction of the product to the market place. The sales force finds that during the time interval from initial survey to product introduction, the desires of the market place have changed dramatically. The features and benefits so carefully researched and designed into this product are either obsolete, not sufficient to satisfy a more mature market, or not what the market wants now. So we repeat the cycle and hope to be more successful the next time.

This approach will not cut it in the current arena of global competition.

What would the RMO approach be to the same situation? The RMO strives to set or exceed customer expectations. In the product design cycle, this desire presents the question, "Why is the new product being designed or an existing product improved through redesign?" The answer: The customer requires it. In other words, we do not generate product speculating that customers will want it. We build the product or provide the service that the market place indicates it wants. This question applies even when we are developing a new market.

How is this focus on the customer different from the traditional, nontime-based approach. While both recognize the importance of the customer, the response-managed approach values speed, which reduces response time. In the response-managed environment, it is important to provide products or services quickly. This will be what your competition will be trying to do. *Quickly* means that we do not have the time to recalibrate the product once we release it to the market place. We do not have the time to get it right the second or third time; we must get it right the first time. We surely do not have either the time or the resources to deliver a product or service after years of development, only to find that it is obsolete as soon as it hits the market place.

How do we avoid these traps? We involve the customers by allowing them to become integral members of the design team. Instead of partitioning functions among engineering, materials, purchasing, market research, manufacturing and other staff, we deliberately bring these functions together into a design team. The design team is responsible for quickly developing a design that can be readily transformed into a manufactured quality product. *All variables that can affect the outcome of the design effort are quickly identified and reconciled on an ongoing basis during the design cycle.*

With this approach, the design team can remain adaptable to changes during the design cycle. If new technology emerges, the team can quickly incorporate it. If customer requirements change as a result of increasing expectations and developments within a market, the emerging product can be altered to remain current. The result is the development, production, and release of products or services that are current, that will be exactly what the market is saying it wants, and that is made available exactly when the market says it wants them.

While changes may occur during the design and development stages, the overall result will be a greatly shorter development time. Not only will it be shorter, but it also ensures that the resources invested in the effort are not wasted by changing market requirements during the development cycle.

Yet another level of benefit is available through this approach: customer loyalty. Which customers will exhibit the greater loyalty to the customer-supplier relationship: the ones who are consulted during a market survey as part of a population sample, or the ones who have been actively engaged on an ongoing basis in the design of products that they feel are being specifically developed for them? The latter customer, of course, will have established a very different relationship with their supplier.

The RMO approach to new product development provides a vital link in the codependent enterprise chain. Supplier and customer are working together to ensure their mutual success in providing products to final customers. Not only is the development cycle shortened, but the resulting products are also supportive of the competitive objectives of chain members. Technology information is shared, capabilities are realistically developed, specifications are achievable, risk is shared, learning and developmental costs are shared, and end users are provided products and services that consistently exceed expectations. Establishing this level of interaction and cooperation between business partners increases each member's ability to effectively compete with those outside the codependent chain. Profit opportunities increase, market share growth is enabled, quality is improved, and costs are diminished.

8

Rethinking the Present... Discovering the Future (Part II)

Quality

If we continue to view quality as the competitive answer to the demands of global competition, many U.S. industries may find that they are producing high-quality buggy whips at a time when everyone else is driving cars. Where *does* the concept of quality fit within a response-managed organization? During the late 1980s and into the 1990s, many U.S. companies have adopted some type of quality-related program. Many companies who have not yet done so expect to move in that direction in the future.

Is quality the magic button that, once pushed, cures all ills? No. Quality is important, but it must be placed in perspective. In most instances, quality is object-related; that is, this "object" is of good quality. It meets specification. In fewer instances, quality is defined as being organizational in nature, affecting everything that we do. In yet other instances, quality is related to the customer's needs. Those adopting this definition frequently identify an external customer and an internal customer within the organization. In this latter context, quality is often product- or service-oriented; we should not provide questionable quality to external or internal customers.

Quality programs have many names, affecting different aspects of corporate quality. Each name is associated with its own definition of quality: statistical process control (SPC), total quality management (TQM), total quality control (TQC), total quality (TQ). Many companies who adopt total quality programs extend their expectations to their vendors, imposing certification requirements to qualify as a supplier. Invariably, certification requires a potential supplier to document the reliability of their manufacturing process.

These approaches to quality miss the point. The only measure of quality of any significance is performance—performance defined by response-managed parameters. All else, while beneficial, is of significantly lesser importance and can divert us from the real issues.

It is not important for a supplier to be capable of producing 100-percent quality products. It is important that the supplier's customers receive only 100-percent quality products. In other words, the ability to respond to customer needs by providing quality services and products is important because it affects the customer.

Further, shifting the emphasis of quality to response adds a final dimension to our quality definitions: purpose. This element answers the all-important question of *why* quality is important and *what* is important about it.

The response dimension allows us to redefine how we approach our customers and use quality to differentiate ourselves from our competition. It allows us to expand what we offer our customers beyond traditional measures of quality products provided at competitive cost. These attributes, as we will see, are no longer special in nature; they are the price of admission to the competitive arena.

The issue of quality is of concern to suppliers who have to maintain a quality presence in their marketplace. Suppliers who do not have processes in place capable of sustaining high levels of quality performance suffer the burden of inspecting bad quality out of product batches prior to shipment to the customer. They need to maintain artificially high finished goods inventory levels to support customer lead time expectations, and require high raw material levels to buffer against planning scheduling and vendor problems. They must maintain high WIP inventory levels to buffer against manufacturing inefficiencies and require additional staffing to smooth out problems to ensure that they are resolved in-house and not by the customer.

All this is of little concern to customers, as long as that supplier is able to consistently respond to their needs in a quality manner.

The response-managed organization would not bear these burdens for very long. Inspection, increased production to cover defect loss, and high inventory levels are all response inhibitors. If an organization wishes to become a response-managed organization, it will eventually have to address these quality-related issues. Response inhibitors inhibit response. They contradict the strategic direction of the response-managed organization. They are dealt with as components of response instead of quality. In this context their importance relative to other response issues may differ among different organizations.

This book defines the principles of response-managed competition. When I discuss these principles with many companies that implemented total quality programs, the discussions share some common attributes. Always prior to my explaining the quality dimension of response-managed competition, I ask for the client's definition of quality. This leads to an explanation that products or services have to be 100 percent according to specification and that they have to meet customer expectations. Their replies never include elements of quality attributed to response-managed competition. Once the response-managed quality issues are outlined, virtually all say that, of course, these issues are included in their quality programs. However, I have yet to meet a "quality"-oriented company that was able to associate these attributes with their quality program prior to my enumerating them.

Defining quality as the attainment of performance levels that meet customer expectations is a very risky proposition. If the best you can do is to meet customer expectations, you leave yourself vulnerable to the competitor who is able to exceed customer expectations and to redefine those expectations. For example, do we really know if our customers order what we want them to or what they would like to? Do our customers base their buying decisions on their historical expectation of our ability to respond to those decisions or on their actual need at the time of purchase?

My experience is that, in most instances, customer expectations reflect historical experience. So, if buyers historically experience six-month lead times when ordering a particular product, their lead time expectation with regard to that product is six months. Planning and purchasing decisions will be based on this expectation.

Should we base our response targets on maintaining this level of performance—six-month lead times? After all, this position would be consistent with meeting customer expectations. The response-managed organization would ask whether the six-month lead time represented historical expectation or desired performance. Remember that one of our tests as a response-managed organization is to ask if the level of performance we provide is consistent with the level of performance we ideally desire from our suppliers. In most instances the ideal level of performance we would like from our suppliers will be significantly different from the six-month expectation. Most companies, when given the choice between extended purchasing lead time and short lead time windows, will choose the short option. As discussed earlier, there is little advantage to long lead times.

The company that sets customer expectation as their barometer of success will be vulnerable to a competitive threat from the company that seeks to provide a level of service similar to what they ideally desire for themselves.

To the response-managed organization, quality extends to embrace the quality of performance and the quality of the relationship between trading partners within a codependent chain. The quality of products and services in general is accepted as an absolute minimum standard of acceptable performance required to be competitive.

No Second Chance

What's important is current capability, not past performance.

When the consumer uses a product provided by a final customer, the success or failure of that product depends on the consumer's perception of that product's quality. If there is any difficulty with the overall performance of the product or service, or with a component of that product or service, the consumer assigns responsibility not to the component, but to the entire product. For example, upon encountering a problem with the car radio, a car buyer will not say, "What a poor radio the supplier made." Instead, the comment will be that, "So-and-so cars have lousy radios." The car manufacturer receives the entire blame for the faulty component. The final customer and the consumer each suffer because of the faulty component. Some companies recognize this relationship and take steps aimed at improving the quality of their products and of the components used in their products. Vendor certification programs come to mind as one way for buyers to strive to ensure the quality of purchased components.

Companies have become more attuned to quality and sophisticated in distinguishing between the price of a good or service and the cost of the items to the organization using them. As a result, they are reducing vendor populations to include only the "good guys." Their reduction process separates the good guys from the not-so-good or bad guys. The challenge for industry is to be classified as one of the good guys. Once the selection is made, the not-so-good guys and bad guys will not get a second chance to compete.

The following table appeared in a 1991 *Wall Street Journal* article. The table gives some indication of the magnitude of change occurring in vendor reduction programs.

	Number of Suppliers		
	Current	Previous	Change (%)
Xerox	500	5,000	−90%
Motorola	3,000	10,000	−70
Digital Equipment	3,000	9,000	−67
General Motors	5,500	10,000	−45
Ford Motor	1,000	1,800	−44
Texas Instruments	14,000	22,000	−36
Rainbird	380	520	−27
Allied-Signal Aerospace	6,000	7,500	−20

Which column, current or previous, will your company be in? Those in the "current" column may look forward to long-term business arrangements with their customers. In addition, they will share in the increased revenues resulting from the distribution of total purchasing dollars among significantly fewer suppliers than before.

What inducement will companies in the "previous" column offer to displace one of the selected "current" companies? I can think of no inducement other than possibly a technological breakthrough. Even then, if the technological breakthrough is the only inducement, without the added benefits provided by the current companies, the breakthrough by itself may not offer enough advantage to cause a change in business partner. In fact, unless such a breakthrough is accompanied by the associated business benefits, the customer would likely work with the current supplier to develop a viable alternative to the new technology.

Companies who do not make the first cut, to become current, may not get a chance to catch up later. The time to act is now. Those who wait are at risk of losing, and losing big. Those who act and act now are "at risk" of being selected as the current supplier and having to deal with increased business opportunity.

This is a fundamental response-managed competition issue. Response-managed organizations are fully aware of this situation and strive to ensure that they are selected to be current instead of previous suppliers. This selection process, when extended throughout the supplier/customer chain, forms the basis for codependent competitive entities. In this environment the maxim is not: "He who laughs last laughs best." The new maxim is: "He who laughs best laughs first."

Rebuilding the Competition

We have established the Japanese as scapegoats, as the excuse for our prevailing economic difficulties, as the source of all our industrial problems. A great deal has been said about the other fellow cheating—as an excuse for marginal U.S. performance. Much has also been written to support the cheating premise: They are government-subsidized. We rebuilt their industries after World War II. Their markets are closed to foreign goods. They cheat. Everything they do they learned from us. They can make great copies but aren't creative.

What happened? At the end of the second world war, the Japanese were devastated. They lost the war, were occupied by Allied troops, and were forced to adopt a democratic form of government in which the emperor would no longer be recognized as a divine leader. The United States, having learned from history, invested in the rebuilding of Japan and helped them to establish a nonmilitary industrial base.

Great achievements were realized during the rebuilding years from 1946 to 1952. The Japanese were recognized as leading the world in the production of carnival amusements. Japanese products were, at best, poor copies of American and European products. "Made in Japan" meant cheap, inexpensive, poor-quality products. They obviously were not cheating in those days. Japan was not a major player in world markets.

How they transformed themselves from the leading junk manufacturers to the leading quality purveyor of goods is a story worth considering. In the early 1950s, the Japanese recognized that they could not compete in world markets. In response, business and government began to collaborate in a national effort to transform the industrial base from carnival supply manufacturers to a leading international industrial nation. Japan, as a nation, adopted an economic growth strategy. In support of this transformation, they relied on information and teaching provided largely by Americans. First, there were Deming and Juran, and then the Japanese visited countless American companies where they were shown how we did it.

They were good pupils. They learned and provided that greatest of all compliments to their teachers; they imitated them. Over the years they transformed the teachers' systems into their own systems, and began not only to overtake their teachers, but to surpass them in virtually all areas of industrial activity.

The transformation took place not so much as a result of our rebuilding efforts, but instead as a result of their efforts to catch up with the rest of the industrialized world. *They invested in the economic growth of their nation.*

Learning from the Students

Now our positions seem to have been reversed. We now accuse our former pupils of cheating. They are not playing fair, we need a level playing field, and so forth. Perhaps now it is time for the teachers to learn from their pupils. We are now the ones who need to adopt a national industrial strategy. We in the United States need to consolidate all sectors of industry and work together in partnership to again regain our former competitive edge. Business, government, labor (union and nonunion), and management, must all unite in achieving a common national goal—the reinvigoration of American industry. We must adopt a national economic growth strategy at least equal to our former national defense strategy. No lesser effort will succeed.

Strategies

Ever since World War II, the United States has been pursuing a national military strategy: to defend ourselves and our allies against a possible attack. During this period, we have based virtually all national decisions on this strategy: We have invested our resources in a strong national defense—our research dollars, our best and brightest minds, our infrastructure decisions, and our legislative efforts. We have been protecting ourselves from an attack by a global adversary, the former U.S.S.R. During this time, those we were protecting, Europe and the Far East, invested their resources in developing economic strategies.

We were each successful. Our military strategy succeeded in defeating the Soviet Union. They went into bankruptcy shortly before we did. The economic strategy adopted by the East and West was also successful, allowing them to surpass us in industry, infrastructure, manufacturing, and education. While we were developing military might, they were developing economic might. While we invested in questionable weapons systems, they invested in educational systems. While we cut back on infrastructure investment, they increased spending to ensure a strong base for their economic future. While we were making the transition from high-paying manufacturing jobs to low-paying low-skill service jobs, they were expanding high-paying, high-skill manufacturing jobs. We were evolving towards third world status while they were growing into economic leaders.

To be sure, much of the growth that occurred in Europe and the East is a result of the purchasing power of the U.S. consumer. Our economic competitors will quickly acknowledge this fact. However, as we continue to lose our high-paying industries and associated jobs, replacing them with low-paying hospitality and service jobs, our position as the largest consumer economy will steadily diminish. The European community is seeking unity and creating a common market, while we flounder without strong leadership hoping that tomorrow, yesterday will return.

The European Economic Community (EEC) represents a potentially larger consumer market than ever existed within the United States alone. As we continue to lose status as a significant world power and the EEC grows, we will see the end of the prosperous America that we and our parents enjoyed. Unless we take action now, the tide of change may pass us by. We may lose the opportunity to regain a position as a leading industrial nation.

Our attempt to establish a North American equivalent to the EEC, the North American Free Trade Agreement, may be a dangerous answer to the competitive challenges we face. On the surface, this agreement seems to describe a market potential significantly greater than the EEC. On the basis of the information available to date [August 1992], I see no basis for unbridled optimism.

Several differences exist between the EEC and NAFTA approaches. In my opinion, three distinct areas of difference are not being adequately considered:

1. The EEC seeks to equalize the competitive playing field among member nations and to allow each to participate according to its ability to contribute to the economic well-being of the community as a whole.

The NAFTA relationship does not appear to strive towards this type of interrelationship among member nations. The NAFTA relationship, instead of striving for equality among participating nations, seems to allow some nations to take advantage of specific areas of inequality such as the labor rate and environmental differentials between Mexico and its Northern partners.

2. The EEC views the entire community as a unified market, and in addition seeks to export products to nonmember states. Member nations are for the most part, developed containing healthy economies in which individuals possess the purchasing power to support a unified market approach.

The NAFTA nations view each other in the same manner but their reality is a little different. The Northern nations, the United States and Canada, currently enjoy certain benefits resulting from a mutually advantageous trade partnership. The view of NAFTA proponents is that the inclusion of Southern hemisphere populations will expand market potentials. Missing from this analysis is the purchasing power potential in this expanded market.

The low labor rates that make the Southern labor force attractive are not sufficient to support significant growth in purchasing ability. In fact, this labor differential may actually result in a diminution of existing purchasing power within the hemisphere. This condition can occur if additional high-paying jobs are transferred to low-wage states. Those receiving the low wages will not be able to purchase the products they are producing. Those who lost their high-paying jobs to the low-wage states will have also lost much or all of their ability to purchase goods and services equal to previous levels. The result will be an overall reduction in purchasing ability within the community as a whole.

3. The EEC seeks to expand exports. The economies possible from their economic union can and most likely will improve their competitive position. If they are allowed to export freely to nonmember nations, they will be positioned to expand their market base.

The NAFTA nations will not enjoy a similar advantage. As already indicated, their internal markets may shrink as wages shrink overall. The market potential of the low-wage nations is marginal at best. What markets will be available to absorb the products produced in the low-wage areas? The EEC comes to mind. Will the EEC be as open in allowing imports as the NAFTA nations? Evidence to date would seem to indicate that they will not be tolerant of uncontrolled imports.

The risk to the United States may be significant. Jobs may be exported in greater numbers than were realized during the 1980s and early 1990s. Purchasing power may be diminished. Tax revenues may be reduced, which will further reduce our ability to be proactive in responding to these competitive challenges.

Those supporting NAFTA would suggest that increases in exported goods will create more jobs lost through the export of jobs. While this may be true, the number of net jobs (those created minus those lost) cannot be very great. The real risk is the possibility that we will experience an overall reduction in standard of living as the U.S. economy is more closely aligned with the Mexican economy. This possibility does not appear to be adequately balanced by the prospect of modest gains in employment.

As a nation we have the capability to surpass any other industrial nation on earth. We have the ability to rise to this present danger and to shape our future. Many American companies have already demonstrated our ability to compete successfully in this emerging global market. Capability is not the issue. The only question before us is, "Do we have the national will to accept this challenge and prevail?"

The Myth About Technology

Scenario: We just spent megabucks to upgrade our capital equipment, laid off half the direct labor force, and increased executive year-end bonus packages. But we still cannot compete with the low-tech guys down the street.

They *must* be cheating. Their equipment is *old.* It was purchased before we even built the new facility. Their labor force is old; half of them were born there. The only thing they know is how to use that old equipment. They couldn't tell you what a five-axis lathe looks like if their lives depended on it. They can't even work independently. They have to keep getting together to decide how to run a job or how to bid on a job. They can't even do that right; they keep underbidding us. Don't they know what production costs are today? They shouldn't even be in business much less taking work away from us. We use the newest, best, biggest, most automated, most expensive technology available today. We're not on the cutting edge. We're waiting for the cutting edge to catch up with us. That's how far ahead we are.

What's the Problem Here?

Did you ever stop to think about what technology does to give us a competitive edge? Is technology by itself the answer? Technology is a component of the solution, but not *the* solution. It offers an edge only when it is proprietary and only then until it is copied by someone else. What will make *our* purchase of available technology better than *their* (our competitors') purchase of the same technology?

Actually, the role of technology is quite complex. If technology were the only answer, there would be no more prosperous and no less prosperous users of the same technology. None would gain market share, and none would lose it. None would make money, and none would make less or lose.

The "old" company in our scenario, may have the competitive advantage. The building and the equipment are most likely paid for, and the labor force is highly skilled in the use of that equipment. They combine their skills and talents to agree on the best way to respond to business needs. With a stable personnel situation, they are not incurring the costs associated with turnover of personnel. (This is not meant to imply that their high-tech competitor is incurring these costs.) Nor are they incurring ongoing training costs to maintain skills. They do not have increased equipment maintenance costs arising from the need to keep up support stores or to train personnel to maintain their high-tech equipment. To be fair, they will not be able to participate in some jobs, jobs in which they will not be competitive. But for jobs they can bid on, the high-tech shop may find that they are not able to compete with them.

Technology, when properly applied as part of an overall business strategy, can provide substantial benefits. In our example, if technology is employed for its own sake, it will usually not provide much benefit. In many instances, technology is the vehicle to achieve such admirable goals as reductions in work force: "This machine is so productive, it takes the place of x workers." Or technology can improve productivity: "This machine is so fast that you can produce parts twice as fast as you did before." This is perhaps good if your business is only to produce those parts, if your material supply can keep pace with the increased demands, and if customer orders equal the new ability to produce. If any of these conditions is not present, then probably the technology is not so good. (All this assumes the technology supplier can maintain part quality and deliver the produced parts to customers in a timely manner.)

Technology + Purpose + Methods = Competitive Advantage

So how does technology fit into the competitive picture? If competitors have equal access to technology, who will gain the competitive advantage? Stealing a phrase from the Perot for President campaign, "The answer is simple": The one who understands how the technology combines with method and purpose can prove to be an unbeatable competitor.

Technology.   There are different types of technology, ranging from multiaxis machining centers to EDI and computerized business applications. (In the next chapter, we discuss many of the different technologies currently available to industry.) In general, technologies fall into two categories: applied and installed (each discussed in the following chapter).

Purpose. I propose response-managed competition as the ultimate purpose for employing technology. Thus you must ask the question, "Will this technology assist in improving my ability to respond? Or will it remove a response inhibitor from my organization?"

Methods. Which organizational and operational methods, combined with the new technology, will enhance the ability to achieve the purpose, for which the technology was aquired in the first place? If the purpose was RMO and the technology was a new CNC machining center, then what methods should be employed in connection with that machining center?

Suppose, the new machine is installed as an island of automation for runing large product lot size runs, so as to minimize the impact of set-up time and to allow the cost of the machine to be allocated across many parts. Will this approach achieve my purpose? Probably not, if the purpose is to achieve RMO capability. However, if the machine center is integrated into a balanced process in which the machining center efficiencies can be used to improve the efficiency of the entire process, then the entire process becomes more responsive and creates a significant competitive advantage. If that process were part of a JIT manufacturing line, then benefits can be realized throughout the line.

An island of automation not only may not provide any competitive advantage, it may actually result in a competitive disadvantage. The equipment costs associated with an island are the same as those when the equipment is a balanced component of a process. If the island approach diverts attention from the issues of process balance and consistency, or if it results in the production of inventory that cannot be immediately consumed by either customers or elsewhere in the process, then a competitive disadvantage will occur. Why? An opportunity is lost or delayed to achieve improved overall production efficiency and to properly utilize all available capacity, labor, and machine. This inefficiency will artificially drive up manufacturing costs, reducing profit opportunity as well as competitive opportunity. If the island approach results in the island's producing more inventory (due to its increased run time efficiency) than can be immediately consumed, then all we have accomplished is to have increased inventory. There is no immediate return for excess inventory other than the opportunity to pay carrying costs, which reduce profit margin opportunities.

These situations are further compounded when equipment is installed in a line in which the other process steps are thrown out of balance by a need to run large lot sizes in order to offset set-up time. This type of situation will reduce efficiency throughout the process, resulting in reduced ability to respond to customer demand.

Overall, technology by itself can be a considerable response inhibitor. The island approach is surely not a response enhancer.

The issue of technology must be viewed from the perspective of the user and in the context of where the technology will be used, why it is being used, and what results are expected from its use. These issues are covered in the following chapter, "Techno-Babble."

9
Techno-Babble

Having discussed the "Myth About Technology," we can enter the realm of techno-babble to discuss the different types of technology available to modern industry. In general, technology can be grouped into two categories: applied and installed. *Applied* technology pertains to changes in procedures, methods, operations, techniques, and so forth. *Installed* technology is more tangible, more physical in nature; it consists of computers, measuring devices, data collection devices, software, and so on. Many different types of installed and applied technologies are available to the modern manufacturer. Response-managed competition is an example of applied technology. The journey to becoming a response-managed organization typically requires a combination of applied and installed technologies.

Installed technology is typically acquired through capital investment. Applied technology costs are depicted and justified indirectly. It is therefore often easier for companies to adopt installed technology than applied technology: "We can justify the purchase of a new piece of equipment; this is budgeted. We cannot justify hiring outside expertise; we have no budget for this." As seen in the "Myth About Technology," one without the other can result in a zero net gain. In most situations, benefit is derived only when installed and applied technology are properly blended.

Technology may or may not enhance your ability to respond. The response-managed organization will develop their own unique approach to incorporating technologies into their day-to-day activities. As they develop this approach, action taken should be evaluated in the context of:

- Will this action improve my ability to respond?
- Will this action eliminate a response inhibitor?
- Will this action contribute to the overall responsiveness of my organization?

This "means" test, which evaluates the impact of technology on response, allows each organization to determine the level and mix of technology most appropriate for them at any given point in time. The means test helps to assess the merits of related technologies to determine which will provide the greatest opportunity and benefit. The existence and availability of technology do not automatically translate into a need to adopt it. What may be beneficial in one situation can be counterproductive in another similar or related situation.

Do applied and installed ever come together? Probably, but so what? Since it is not important to draw this distinction, why should anyone care? For example, suppose an organization is adopting new methods (converting current practices to response-managed competitive practices), at the same time adopting applied technology. During their transition process, they find it necessary to physically change how various functions perform their day-to-day tasks; they physically alter their environment. Is this physical alteration an example of installed technology? No. While they have physically altered their environment, they have not introduced any new technology into that environment, other than the applied technology that provided the reason for alteration. If, however, they introduce new computer systems to support the physically altered department's functions, they would be mixing applied and installed technology to transform a department. The new computer system is an example of installed technology.

Every area of technology is in a state of continual change. New methods continue to evolve and are developed. Installed technological advances occur daily, far outstripping the ability of most industries to keep pace.

Installed Technology

In our current industrial climate, installed technology relies heavily on emerging computer-based applications. The computer applications are used to manage, monitor, and control, as well as to enhance decision speed and quality. Computer applications can be process- and equipment-based, or they can be associated with various types of information systems. The following is a brief overview of several examples of installed technology.

Computer-Aided Drafting (CAD), Computer-Aided Machining (CAM), Computer-Aided Engineering (CAE). These systems, when properly used, can greatly increase the productivity and quality of engineering activities. Significant benefit can be derived when these technologies are combined with other emerging technologies which allow for easy conversion of computer-generated designs to physical wax- or resin-based models.

When combined with appropriate applied technology, such as a design for manufacturability as an approach to designing new products or components, significant advantage can be gained. The design cycle can be compressed, the quality of the resulting design will be improved, and post-design engineering changes can be reduced or eliminated, except for product improvements resulting from improvements to manufacturing process or based on the availability of new materials or equipment.

Combining these techniques with other installed technologies, such as manufacturing management software, can provide further benefit. For example, a problem confronting many companies—small companies in particular—is their inability to enter into existing markets. Companies wishing to enter mature markets are often confronted with unpleasant choices, one of which is the need to find a way to offset what can be a substantial up-front charge to cover product design efforts. Such companies are typically competing against mature engineering groups and products, for which the engineering development costs have been either recovered or distributed across a volume of product sold. The in-place company will have developed a product price level that reflects this state. The new entrant is forced to determine how to handle the engineering costs associated with developing a competitive product for this market.

The new entrant cannot reasonably expect the market to be willing to pay more for their product to offset their engineering costs. This is especially true when the new company is not redefining the standard of quality or capability available within an industry. Instead, many companies strive to develop products that are similar in capability and price to existing market standards. Their problem results from their inability to recover their development costs through product pricing initiatives.

The application of engineering-related installed and applied technologies can result in a significant reduction in costs associated with product development efforts. This reduction comes primarily from the ability of these technologies to reduce the time it takes to achieve acceptable results. As time is reduced, so are associated costs for labor, materials, and overhead.

Computer-Integrated Manufacturing (CIM). CIM involves both applied and installed technology. The installed components of CIM can cover a lot of ground. Throughout the five-level CIM model, one can find numerous examples of installed technology. At level 1, the equipment itself represents an example of installed technology.

The equipment itself offers many other examples of installed technology, ranging from performance measuring devices designed to capture equipment operating characteristics dynamically (while the equipment is in operation), to automated measurement devices installed on the equipment to capture production quality information and to allow real time control of a process. These devices can be used to transmit information to or receive instructions from the next level of the CIM model, level 2.

Level 2 of the CIM model identifies the programmable logic control (PLC) computers, which are used to monitor and manage equipment performance. PLCs pick up and receive information directly from the equipment they are managing, as well as from the operators operating the equipment in question. PLCs are capable of managing and controlling a process, as well as maintaining tolerances within the boundaries established for the system under control. PLCs receive instructions from and transmit data to the next level of the CIM model, level 3.

Level 3 of the model is associated with the installed technology used as an interface between level-4 systems and level-2 PLCs. At level 3 we find process monitoring and control systems. Typically, these systems will receive operating instructions from the level-4 manufacturing planning systems and relay those instructions to the level-2 PLCs, which will in turn manage the operation of their respective equipments. Level-3 technology is capable of receiving and downloading machine operation settings such as speeds, feed rates, tool selection, and so forth. Level-3 technology is also capable of monitoring equipment performance characteristics and comparing those characteristics to predefined operational standards, communicating new instructions to the level-2 PLCs as needed. In the interaction between the monitoring and control functions, the level-3 technology will manage the level-1 equipment through the level-2 technology, the PLC. Adjustments can be made dynamically to maintain equipment operation within upper and lower control limits. Different levels of alarming signals can be invoked up to automatic machine or process shutdown if operation cannot be maintained within predefined parameters.

Many level-3 systems also support statistical process control (SPC) data collection and analysis. Because these systems monitor operational characteristics in real time, they are also capable of organizing the characteristics into formats appropriate to SPC analysis. This use is a logical extension of their monitoring capabilities.

Level 4 of the model pertains to the manufacturing management systems, which are used to plan, schedule, and manage production. Typical of a level-4 system are MRPII or JIT software systems; these systems contain the instruction sets that are downloaded to the level-3 process monitoring and control systems.

Level 5, the final level, defines the corporate business planning systems. These systems may or may not communicate with the level-4 operating systems.

Equipment operating under the supervision of well defined CIM parameters is capable of producing and delivering consistent quality at optimum productivity levels. A properly designed and maintained CIM environment is capable of sustaining high levels of performance, attaining levels of consistency and uniformity beyond that found in similar non-CIM environments.

Flexible Manufacturing Systems (FMS), and Large Scale FMS (LSFMS).   In the typical FMS, equipment is self-contained and not dependent on human operators to sustain production. FMSs can be remotely controlled, either through control room facilities or by remote control over phone lines using modem interfaces. FMSs can be extended to encompass an entire manufacturing facility. When all manufacturing functions are performed by FMSs, we will have potentially developed a black factory, so named because they can run in the dark. The only humans required are maintenance personnel necessary to ensure the continued operation of the equipment. Machines do not need light to see by as do humans, hence the term *black factory*.

World-Class Manufacturing Support Technology.   Adopting a definition of world-class that is associated with just-in-time manufacturing and operations practices. Several categories of installed technology can be found to support the JIT operations. Examples of this technology would include new ways to handle and move materials through the manufacturing process and to the manufacturing process. Various material tracking systems, such as single- or multiple-card Kanbans, are other examples of supporting installed technology. The many ways in which a need for material can be communicated to material handlers—lights, cards, audible signals, and the like—are all examples of installed technology elements in the JIT environment.

The thrust of these technologies is to improve an ability to move product through a manufacturing process (there are equivalents in the administrative realm). Material flows should be designed to improve the ability of material handlers to respond to the resupply needs of material consumers.

Lasers.   Lasers can be found in many installed technology situations. They can be used to measure and maintain position, to measure size and compare measurement to specification, to measure speed and to gather information used elsewhere within an organization. Lasers can be used in cutting materials, in creating seals, and in laser machining operations.

CNC Machines. This equipment reflects the merging of traditional machinery with computer-based control capabilities. CNC-based equipment provides levels of accuracy, speed, automation, and quality greater than was possible with traditional mechanical and manual equipment.

The impact of CNC technology on responsiveness can be dramatic. A comparison between a traditional screw machine and a CNC lathe highlights the contribution of CNC technology in turning operations. Numerous turning jobs, currently done using screw machines, can also be done on a CNC lathe. The differences between these two approaches can be seen in several areas. For example, screw machines are notorious in requiring long set-up time (typically measured in hours) to change from one job to another. As a result, screw machines are not effective in supporting either job diversity or small manufacturing lot sizes. On the other hand, CNC lathes are capable of supporting rapid change-over between jobs (measured in minutes not hours) and of economically running smaller lot sizes.

The screw machine provides exactly the level of performance incompatible with response. Too many response inhibitors are associated with its use: set-up time, large lot sizes required to distribute the cost of set-up among more stuff, less flexibility, poor use of time, which is used to produce stuff that customers do not need. This time cannot simultaneously be used to produce something that customers need now. Many more examples of response inhibitors are associated with screw machines.

The CNC machine imposes none of these response inhibitors. Instead, it provides the potential for removing these inhibitors from operations.

Assorted Other Machining Methods. Examples are water jet, laser machining, electrodischarge machining (EDM), electrochemical machining (ECM), laser beam cutting (LBC).

Automated Guided Vehicles (AGVs). When judiciously used, AGVs can provide significant benefit. When it is not possible to physically reengineer existing operations with the result that materials have to be moved between physically separated work centers, AGVs can provide a rapid and efficient means for traversing these distances.

Conveyors. An alternative to AGVs, conveyors are currently available in sufficient diversity to support virtually any material handling need faced by modern industry. However, not all situations are suitable for the use of AGVs.

There is also a potential downside if we are not careful in how conveyors are employed. The goal is to reduce material movement to a minimum. If fixed-length conveyors are introduced into a manufacturing process, they tend to institutionalize the travel distance they are bridging. "We designed this terrific conveyor system. It was horribly expensive. Now you want me to redesign it or, even worse, move activities so close to each other as to eliminate it entirely. How do you expect me to justify this?"

The proper use of conveyors and AGVs can provide considerable advantage in a response-managed situation.

Computer-Automated Inspection (CAI) Systems. These types of systems include technology such as automated statistical process control data collection and analysis equipment, nondestructive testing systems, automated measurement systems, and various types of visioning and positioning systems. These applications can be installed in on-line or off-line situations.

Information Systems. Growing in importance, information systems provide a means of linking many differing types of automation into a cohesive whole. One example of this is a CIM environment. Information systems ultimately provide a foundation for building information requirements. We can identify several standard components of our information system:

1. *Computers.* We would expect to install two basic types of computer in our information environment: transaction-driven computers and real time computers. *Transaction-driven computers* typically handle day-to-day business needs including purchase or-

ders, sales orders, and work orders. Our business software runs on transaction-driven computers. The other type of computer, *real time computer*, is not to be confused with the transaction-driven computer, which operates in a real time mode. Real time computers are used to monitor and control equipment. The programmable logic controllers found on different equipments are examples of real time computers.

2. *Different ways to connect computers.* Computers can be linked together several different ways. Two examples are local area networks (LANs) and wide area networks (WANs). *Local area networks* can be used to link several types of computers into a cohesive data network, in which users are provided access to information sourced from several different points along the network. Typically, LANs are employed when the distances between data collection and access devices are not great, such as within a building or facility. *Wide area networks* are similar to LANs, except that they are designed to support the transmission of data across greater distances than LANs.

3. *Different ways for computers to gather information.* We can use several different devices to input data into our computers: Optical scanning, keyboards, bar coding, and magnetic input devices are the most commonly used input devices. While keyboards represent the most prevalent method for entering data into the computer, optical scanning is growing in popularity. With optical scanning, it is possible to directly scan printed, written or photographic documents into a computer. Documents entered through scanning can subsequently be included with other data, transmitted to other interested parties using E-Mail, and altered using appropriate available software designed for this purpose. Bar coding affords the user an easy, accurate way to capture data and to enter that data into the computer. The use of bar coded labels on packaging containers and on identification tags grows each day. Bar coded employee identification badges provide an easy, efficient means for employees to enter time and attendance information, as well as shop-floor-related information, into the computer. Magnetic badges can perform the same functions as bar coded badges.

Bar coding and magnetic encoding are common technologies in use throughout our society. Perhaps the most obvious use of bar codes can be found in grocery stores, where all items on the shelves are identified with a bar coded UPC, which is scanned at the checkout counter. Magnetic encoding is even more prevalent. A visible example of this technology can be found on the back of any credit card. Virtually all credit cards contain a magnetic stripe that can be read electronically when passed through a magnetic reader. The stripe contains identifying information, specific to each card holder.

4. *Specific function computer software.* There are almost an un-limited number of different software packages available to answer any business need. Software can be obtained to operate on different computers, performing specific functions, to support diverse busi-ness needs. Among the more common softwares are manufacturing support packages such as Manufacturing Resource Planning II (MRPII) and just-in-time (JIT), as well as data collection support packages such as those that enable the entry of bar coded data or optical character recognition (OCR), software to support optical scanning. Also, different types of shop floor software packages are available to support computer-integrated manufacturing (CIM) or to drive machine programmable logic controllers.

Virtually any business need can be met with an off-the-shelf software package.

The preceding list is but a sampling of available installed technol-ogy. Fortunately, the list of available technologies grows larger with each passing day. The competitive challenge confronting modern companies is how to select the installed technology that is best for them and then to successfully employ that technology. The re-sponse-managed means test provides a yardstick by which this decision can be evaluated.

Applied Technology

Let us now explore some of the applied technologies available to support modern industry. Applied technology, even more so than installed technology, is too often viewed as being "the" solution to business woes. Applied technologies sweep through the business community like waves. Take, for example, the total quality management (TQM) frenzy sweeping across American industry. Companies large and small are adopting some version of TQM. Not too many years ago, however, the solution was MRPII, then quality circles, then just-in-time, then computer-integrated manufacturing, then statistical process control, and so on. Today, we have sought the solution and—behold!—it is TQM.

Once more we wave the magic wand of business advantage and wonder where our incantation failed. Our competition remains unvanquished.

Response-managed business draws on attributes present in many technologies, on the assumption that there is no one universal right answer. There is only a universal purpose—response—which can be used to determine "your" right answer. We can draw from many applied technologies when developing our individual response-managed strategies. The following are a sampling of current applied technologies:

Total Quality Management (TQM). An outgrowth of the statistical process control movement, TQM extends quality principles throughout an organization. The thrust of TQM is to recognize that quality performance is of equal importance to quality product. Several attributes are commonly associated with a TQM program, among which are high-performance teams, continuous improvement, participative management, benchmarking, and reengineering. TQM programs strive to identify value-adding and nonvalue-adding activities for the purpose of reducing the nonvalue-adding actions.

A response-managed strategy draws on TQM principles. In this book, I speak extensively about the benefits of high-performance teams, of continuous improvement, and of reengineering daily activities. RMO downplays benchmarking as an activity that contributes little towards improvement. RMO redefines the role of management and the nature of their participation in daily business activities.

Response-managed competition adds the missing element of purpose to TQM. It answers the questions, "Why should I adopt elements of TQM, and how should I adopt those elements?" In a sense, TQM is focused on doing things "right," while response-managed competition focuses on also doing things "well." In this context, *right* is quantitative in nature; it relies heavily on baselines and performance measures for validation. *Well* is qualitative in nature; results are important in and of themselves instead of as relative measures. Action is taken because it will provide benefit, not because it is tangible and subject to measurement.

A major difference between TQM and RMO can be seen in the context of something like the Baldridge Award, which total quality management-oriented organizations vie to earn. Some will invest so much time, materials, and resources that they will earn the award but end up filing Chapter 11 because they have not won the competitive battle in their marketplace. Others have won the award and then suspended many of the activities required to win the award. Yet others have won the award only to find that they then had to lay off tens of thousands of workers because the award did not help them win the competitive battles.

The response-managed organization views the award in the context of response: "Will striving for the award increase my ability to respond to the needs of the marketplace and, as a result, become more competitive and profitable? Will the award remove response inhibitors from my environment?" If the striving and attainment of the award will not achieve these objectives, the RMO will not seek the award.

To the response-managed organization, excellence is what they achieved yesterday; tomorrow they will try to do better.

Statistical Process Control (SPC). SPC, a powerful tool when used properly, assumes that all things are quantifiable and can be reduced to examination statistically. The ability to statistically examine a process or activity to gain understanding of how it works, to identify which of its elements can vary, and which elements are stable can be invaluable in improving the performance of the process.

The difficulty of SPC lies not in its methodology but in its implementation. In too many instances SPC is viewed as *the* solution to achieving quality. In these types of situations, SPC techniques are employed to solve most problems, even those that do not require or benefit from this type of approach. Many of the daily problems are such that all the people involved know what they are, know when they will occur, know what will happen once they do occur, and know what has to be done to correct them. What they do not have is the ability or authorization to do what is necessary to correct the problems. Analyzing this type of problem using SPC techniques does not contribute value toward the solution of the problem.

SPC however, has its place. In many process situations, SPC techniques provide the only way to determine the true cause of a problem. SPC can provide insight into darkness and help us to distinguish between cause and effect. When used for these purposes, SPC is valuable and powerful.

Several SPC techniques are routinely used in a response-managed environment: fishbone charts, pareto distributions, and, in appropriate instances, control charts. Unfortunately, other SPC techniques may have to be adopted because they are required by trading partners, various process documentation requirements, provision of cp and cpk ratings, and so forth. This latter situation, the need to document excellence as a means of confirming what we have been doing, is an offshoot of TQM; the idea is that, if our performance measures are good, then our performance will be good. Conversely, the thinking is that somehow it is not enough for just performance to be good as measured by our ability to support customers; unless the statistics supporting that performance are equally good, we are suspect of being less than adequate.

Just-In-Time (JIT).   JIT is a very powerful business tool that, when properly employed, can provide significant competitive benefit and advantage. Just-in-time is also a very misunderstood technology. Several components of JIT, for example, have become synonymous with JIT: continuous flow manufacturing, kanban, single minute exchange of dies (SMED), and cellular manufacturing. Further, many organizations have limited this powerful manufacturing practice to just-in-time inventory. They have transformed supersonic transport into a Piper Cub. JIT is not an inventory reduction system. JIT is an operational method by which manufacturing activities are rearranged into very efficient, flexible, productive entities capable of outperforming all other manufacturing methods. (The exception to this is the so-called black factory, the fully automated factory capable of outperforming typical JIT-based manufacturing operations.)

The utilization of JIT techniques to reengineer manufacturing is a powerful tool used by the response-managed organization. For example, the 5-percent rule is an outgrowth of JIT. Response-managed competition principles further apply the 5-percent rule throughout the organization, not just on the shop floor. The foundation of JIT is to transform manufacturing into a responsive enterprise. JIT environments enjoy greatly reduced manufacturing cycle times, compared to their more traditional batch-oriented counterparts. Reorganization of manufacturing operations into cells is one example of how traditional shop floor workflows can be reengineered for response. Response-managed organizations strive to transform the entire organization into a "response-capable" enterprise.

JIT methodology also embraces several product design technologies. The basis for JIT design is to produce products that can be efficiently manufactured in a JIT manufacturing environment. This type of design effort results in reduced design cycle time, a reduction in engineering changes to released products needed to make them manufacturable, and product design that is more consistent with manufacturing ability. In general, the varying design approaches are aimed at ensuring a close cooperation between design engineers and manufacturing personnel. This is an attempt to do it right the first time—or at least to do it better. Some of the names associated with JIT design technology are design for manufacture, concurrent engineering, simultaneous engineering, and design for assembly (DFA).

Response-managed design employs JIT methodology and extends the design team concept outward to include vendors and customers as active participants in the design process. Product design "teams" replace the solitary design engineer(s). (The issue of response-managed design has been addressed throughout the book; see "It Took So Long to Design That It's Obsolete," Chap. 7.)

Group Technology.   "Getting the most from the least," group technology adherents strive to create the greatest number of end items using the fewest components. Effort is made to create standard components and manufacturing operations. In this environment items are arranged into groups, and groups of items can be associated with predefined manufacturing routing operations. Thus, when a new item is introduced, an appropriate routing can be generated quickly once the group for the item is known.

"Getting the most from the least," also pertains to *how* components are used. The intent is to find ways to combine standard components into the greatest number of different end items as possible—to use what is available, when possible, instead of artificially creating a new part number. For example, group technology can also be used to improve operational efficiency by grouping parts by the tool set on a CNC machine, to minimize set-up and tool changeover time.

Too often, the systems we use to evaluate engineering contribution is based on the idea that engineers are supposed to be creative. Creativity is measured by their ability to conjure up new part numbers, which can be combined into new end items. Thus, the more part numbers engineers create, the more creative they are and the more reward we will provide. Never mind that the "new" bracket is not necessary, that we could just as well have used the old one instead of moving the mounting holes a few micromillimeters and giving it a new part number. This type of creativity is destructive. Not only do we have a new part number, we also have to retool to make this part. Further, we have the "opportunity" to make and store more inventory items. Of course, the need to maintain stock to support product field maintenance can be overlooked since these parts make money for us. ("Right!")

The response-managed organization will use group technology techniques as often as possible because they definitely can improve response capability and eliminate response inhibitors.

Electronic Data Interchange (EDI). One of the most powerful response enhancing tools available today, EDI has had a dramatic impact on modern business. Virtually *all* aspects of business endeavor are affected by EDI. EDI is the electronic standard for business documents using standard formats. EDI allows business communications, which previously took days to weeks of time, to be accomplished in minutes. EDI replaces conventional mail, of all types, with an electronic equivalent that can be delivered at the speed of electricity. Send the document for receipt within minutes, anywhere in the world serviced by an appropriate electronic mail service. In EDI parlance, the electronic mail services are called *value-added networks (VANs)*.

EDI offers producers numerous benefits. It is capable of eliminating numerous response inhibitors, both direct inhibitor delays caused by a delay in information flow and indirect inhibitors, such as those resulting from errors in data or information flow. Properly used, EDI can reduce manufacturing cycle time, improve inventory mix, expand purchasing lead time, improve product quality, enhance competitive position with customers, improve communication with suppliers, and provide enhanced profit opportunity to both trading partners in the EDI chain. These are only a few of the benefits possible.

The response-managed organization will use EDI to great advantage. EDI supports internal process reengineering and cycle time reduction efforts, as well as improved coordination between members of a codependent chain. It can assist in reducing engineering cycle time and will overall, even if only used in a limited way, improve organizational response time.

Preventative/Predictive Maintenance (PM) and Total Productive Maintenance (TPM). At last, maintenance is gaining recognition as an important element in achieving performance excellence. Maintenance is an especially vital link in the response-managed chain. Response-managed organizations have choices to make determining how to perform maintenance: They can choose an "It-ain't-broke-don't-fix-it" approach, dealt with earlier in this book, or they can choose a more productive approach, such as preventative or predictive maintenance (PM). The PM approach places emphasis on response by recognizing the inability of equipment to produce product at the same time as it is down for maintenance. In the PM approach, downtime is managed so that it does not interfere with planned production time. This approach increases productive uptime and better supports operational stability, reliability, and response capability.

Response-managed organizations will support maintenance efforts with the same enthusiasm as they support any other business function. In the response-managed environment, the maintenance function is viewed as a partner in achieving excellence instead of as a necessary evil. If you wish to make quality products and to perform at response-managed levels, you must develop and implement response-managed maintenance practices.

Activity-Based Costing. As manufacturing practices change to become more efficient and responsive, the traditional full absorption accounting methods become less relevant in accurately describing costs. (The section, "The Accounting Trap," in Chap. 7, explores this situation in greater depth.) New cost accounting practices are called for, one of which is activity-based accounting.

In the activity-based world, cost is apportioned to products based on the actual amount of activity invested in that product. If, for example, the cost of purchasing a component would depend partly on how much of the purchase process was actually invested in the purchase of the product. We would not just accumulate the total purchase cost and assign a percentage of that cost to each product purchased. Perhaps one product requires extensive market research prior to being purchased, while another product needs no market research. If all other factors are equal, the product requiring the market research receives a greater share of the purchasing cost than the product that does not require research. Each of these products are costed on the basis of the value of the activities actually invested in their purchase.

The preceding are representative examples of currently available applied technologies. In some instances, a technology can fall into both categories (installed and applied). A good example of this is EDI. The applied portion of EDI is represented by the change in operations required by a conversion to EDI communication between trading partners. The ability to communicate in EDI requires that we utilize installed technologies to support that communication.

The competitive challenge facing those seeking to adopt applied technologies is the same as that for installed technology: how to select which applied technology is best for them and then to successfully employ that technology. As always, the response-managed means test provides a yardstick for this decision.

Closing Thoughts on Technology

Response and technology go together. I can think of no instance in which some application of technology, either applied or installed, would not improve response. Choosing the correct mix of technology is, however, another story, even using the response means test.

An Illustrative Problem

The challenge is to select the best approach to technology between two companies; one is a very large repetitive manufacturing company, the other a relatively small company. Each is looking at similar technology. The large company produces a diverse assortment of products; the smaller company produces only components to be used in assemblies produced by other companies. The large company is in the process of installing pull-driven, balanced, manufacturing assembly lines. The small company is seeking to improve their ability to respond to customer requests. The equipment under review is a CNC lathe.

Which of these two would benefit more from the use of *high-productivity automation (HPA)*, which is installed technology capable of producing product at high speed and in quantity? Which would benefit more from the use of *low-productivity automation (LPA)*, which is similar to HPA but less automated, slower, and generally much less expensive?

The Right (?) Answer

Perhaps the right answer is that the smaller company will be better off with the high-productivity automation, while the large company will be better off with the low-productivity automation. In the small company, the introduction of HPA can have the effect of increasing productive capacity. Their product mix is small, with only a few products running in stand-alone mode. They are not assembling products; they are producing components. High-productive automation can provide them a level of speed, repeatability, quality, and automation beyond their current capability.

The larger company will be better off with the low-productivity automation. Since they are in the process of installing balanced pull lines, line balance is of particular importance to them. In their situation, we would probably find that the run speed of the high-productivity automation will be significantly faster than its preceding and following operations. If so, then the HPA machine could not be reasonably balanced with the rest of the line. It would consume the products from preceding operations too rapidly for them to keep up, and would thus be unable to sustain production, experiencing lots of idle time. The large company would be unable to benefit from the high-productivity potential of the equipment. In addition, they would pay a premium for a theoretical level of productivity that they could not enjoy. It would not be feasible to balance the rest of the line with the productivity of the high-productivity equipment.

A better solution for the large company would be to take advantage of the cost differential between the high-productivity solution and the low-productivity solution, perhaps acquiring more than one low-productivity piece of equipment. (The low-productivity machines cost significantly less than the high-productivity equipment.) Our large company could buy several of the low-tech machines for the price of one high-productivity machine. The purchase of several machines, instead of just one, allows the large company to install each smaller machine as a dedicated machine in a specific manufacturing line. This approach can lead to reduced or even eliminated set-up time and to greater overall efficiency.

In this example, the larger company would be better off with the lesser technology. The smaller company would receive greater benefit from the more productive technology.

Does our answer to the problem agree with our technology formula?

Technology + Purpose + Methods = Competitive advantage

You decide!

The Large Company

The technology. A fully automated CNC machining center.

The purpose. To become a response-managed organization.

The method. To use the technology in a balanced pull line configuration.

The Small Company

The technology. A fully automated CNC machining center.

The purpose. To improve their ability to respond to customer requests.

The method. To establish a highly automated machining center.

10
Case Studies:
It Really Works

The companies in these case studies have little in common other than a desire to lead in their marketplaces and to clearly distinguish themselves from their competition. They have each adopted response-managed principles as the foundation on which to achieve their objectives.

The companies provide diversity in management style, products, industry type, size, and application of response-managed principles. Management styles range from moderately authoritarian to total team-oriented decision-driven management. Products cover many different industries—heavy industry through light manufacturing. Industry types include repetitive manufacturing, configure-to-order manufacturing, repetitive job shop, one-of-a-kind job shop manufacturing, and combinations of these. Company sizes range from small (with annual sales revenues below $15 million per year) to very large (with sales volumes approaching $100 million per year or more).

Response-managed organizations can come in all shapes, types, and sizes. There is no threshold below or above which it is not feasible to be response-managed. These following companies serve as examples of how particular response-managed elements have been employed to great advantage. They constitute a parade of excellence.

The "Bull's-Eye" Principle: The MART

The MART corporation manufactures high-pressure industrial washing machines for cleaning metal products. The MART product is considered the Cadillac of washers, offering customers unique features and benefits. The MART is a relatively small company, under $15 million a year in sales.

The MART takes prides in being able to respond to diverse customer needs. The company is organized so as to ensure their ability to produce not only their standard products but also to efficiently meet the very special custom needs of their customers.

Their approach to engineering customer "specials" is based on the use of existing technology whenever possible, combined with a creative design team that develops the necessary new technology. New technology is developed in such a way as to allow, to the greatest extent possible, the new developments created for one customer to be absorbed into existing products as product improvements. This approach ensures that their products remain "current" and that they continue to lead their competition in product performance. Their commitment to continuous product improvement leads them to seek new and creative ways to improve their product line. They are eager to partner with customers to develop new solutions to individual customer needs.

The MART establishes clearly defined goals and is able to set accurate targets. They can identify their bullseye. As an example, the early 1990s represented a period of transition and growth for The MART. During a time when the economy was generally sluggish, they were able to grow at a considerable rate. Their growth was a direct result of a management decision to adopt profit improvement programs that called for an investment in growth. During the recessionary times they invested in future growth. When most companies were withdrawing from markets, reducing staff, or otherwise cutting costs, they invested. These actions allowed them to prosper during recessionary times and to build a foundation for continued future growth.

During this time they invested in hiring new staff to expand departments thereby improving their ability to respond to customer demand. For example, the project engineering staff was expanded and the 1992 project engineering budget was increased by 217 percent over the 1991 budget. They also invested in manufacturing operations, increasing shop floor staff and equipment to be able to respond to customer delivery schedules. As a result, they were able to earn business for which customers were willing to pay a premium for rapid delivery of products.

Were they rewarded for their efforts? During 1992 (hardly a time of dynamic economic growth), they increased sales by 35.8 percent. At the same time, they reduced the cost of sales by 4.4 percent and increased net profit by 3.6 percent over the preceding year. As a result of their profit improvement goals, they were able to increase gross margin by 6.3 percent. During this same period they reduced customer service expenses by over 44 percent and reduced warranty service expenses by 53 percent. As a result of the changes made to administrative processes, they were able to increase administrative support staff while reducing overall administrative expenses by more than 15 percent.

The MART believes that they must provide quality products to their markets. It is the view of the company president, Gary Minkin, that each MART product must contribute to existing technology in their marketplace. They truly wish to be the standard against which other similar companies are measured.

One of the best ways to represent how The MART approaches day-to-day operations is represented by a story that Mr. Minkin tells. It is his "Roger Bannister" story:

QUESTION: Before, 19__, how many runners ran the mile in less than four minutes? This is a no-brainer. The answer is none. Why not?

ANSWER: Because all runners knew that it was not possible to run the mile in less than four minutes. All of those associated with running knew that it was impossible to run a four-minute mile. Since everyone *knew* that breaking the four-minute mile limit was impossible, no one attempted to run that fast. After all, it was impossible. Instead of striving to do what all agreed could not be done, runners set their sights on excelling in what could be done.

QUESTION: Today, how many runners run the mile in less than four minutes?

ANSWER: Virtually all serious milers run a three-plus-minute mile. Running a four-minute mile is not enough if one wishes to compete in the international racing community.

MORAL: As long as we focus on what cannot be done, we will never experience the elation that comes from achieving excellence. We will have to instead be content with our excuses, explaining why we were not able to compete.

Roger Bannister did not recognize the four-minute mile limit as a limit. He approached the challenge of running faster than a four minute as a challenge, something that could be achieved. Once the self-imposed, artificial limit on achievement was removed, there was no way to predict what a runner was capable of accomplishing. There were no limits; there was only effort to excel. (By the way, Gary tells the story in a much better fashion than I was able to convey by writing it.)

The Roger Bannister story is important for its ability to vividly and graphically demonstrate what can happen if we set our sights beyond the boundaries of conventional wisdom. Who knows what can be accomplished once we stop telling ourselves what we cannot do and begin to explore the boundaries of what we might be able to do—if only we dare?

The story of The MART is an example of the Roger Bannister story. They dared to be different and to act contrary to conventional wisdom. They invested and grew when conventional wisdom would have been to consolidate, contract, and wait out the "bad" times. The MART was not ready to accept advice telling them what they could not do. Instead, they explored the boundaries of what might be and won.

The Question of Response: The XYZ Story

XYZ company prefers to remain anonymous, but the events are nonetheless real. XYX is one of several similar facilities, located throughout the United States, that can be classified as heavy industry. The products made at these facilities are similar, each facility having its own throughput capacity. Our XYZ facility is thesmallest of the group in physical size, throughput capacity, and staffing. XYZ employs about 85 people and has annual sales of about $120 million.

The separate facilities share common problems: equipment uptime, maintenance effectiveness, finished goods inventory, meeting customer ship schedule requirements, maintaining quality standards. Quality standards are particularly rigorous. The nature of their product is such that product consistency and uniformity are critical and product standards have to be repeatable over many years. Equipment uptime and maintenance are continual problems. Production requirements are such that their manufacturing support equipments are continually under stress. Their manufacturing is batch process in nature, although they are not a process manufacturing environment. When one part of their facility goes out of service, it can affect several associated process steps. Maintenance activities were traditional, with maintenance and production competing for access to production equipment. Production schedules were established both to produce to customer order and to build finished goods inventory levels. The production process was divided into two distinct activities: One produced a subassembly, which was placed in inventory: the other finished the subassembly, converting it into a finished product. There were several specific subassemblies, each capable of being converted into multiple end items. Customer ship schedule requirements were ambitious, placing demands on production.

Prior to the conversion to response-managed principles, all facilities operated in the same manner. In fact, each adopted similar approaches to technology, applied and installed. My involvement began when they decided to improve on maintenance activities by implementing a computerized maintenance system. The maintenance system was the same for each facility: the implementation of that system was not.

In all instances, the implementation process provided an opportunity to use the maintenance system as a basis for adopting response-managed principles. Each facility decided how they were going to use the maintenance system to their specific advantage, even though each was faced with the same maintenance problem—too much equipment downtime. In general, their prior maintenance practices were traditionally primitive. Maintenance was performed on the basis of "he who screams loudest gets service." Supporting equipment documentation was nonexistent; there was no maintenance planning function. Maintenance stores were in a state of disarray, with each facility maintaining several maintenance parts storage warehouses—some indoors, others outdoor locations with parts stored in fields. Inventory was managed using a manual locater and balance card system. There were no formal preventative or predictive maintenance programs. An informal oil, lube, and inspect system was the extent of their PM system.

Production personnel were continually complaining about the quality of maintenance and about the continual equipment downtime. There was virtually no communication among different functional groups.

Of all the facilities, the XYZ plant decided to approach maintenance differently. XYZ decided to use the maintenance system as an excuse to address many organizational problems within the facility. XYZ had decided to become response-managed in organization and operation.

The implementation approach used at XYZ was similar to that outlined in Chap. 2, "Starting the Transformation." A Project Team was formed, and a steering committee was identified. The project team undertook the task of developing an implementation plan that touched on all areas of plant activity.

Several specific recommended and adopted actions had a profound affect on the daily performance levels achieved at the plant:

1. A maintenance planner position was created. All maintenance activities would be coordinated and authorized by the planner.

2. A formal Production/Maintenance planning meeting was instituted. This meeting was held at least once each week. During the meeting, Maintenance and Production scheduled equipment downtime and specific maintenance activities to be performed during the downtime.

3. Inventory procedures were developed, along with ways to eliminate the time spent looking for material.

4. All equipment located at the facility was documented and described in bill-of-material format.

5. Communication between corporate and plant engineering departments was improved.

6. New procedures and policies were developed, covering all aspects of plant activity.

These are a sample of the types of changes instituted, not a complete list.

As a result of these changes several things happened. XYZ discovered *when less is more and when more is less*. More maintenance resulted in less downtime. Less downtime resulted in more production time.

One of the biggest hurdles was the barrier between Production and Maintenance. Each was at war with the other. A perpetual tug-of-war state existed over who would have access to the equipment. With the intervention of the plant manager, an individual of unusual courage and conviction, the decision was made to schedule production downtime to increase maintenance access to the equipment. Initially, this decision was resisted by Production management who insisted that they would be unable to meet production demands if their equipment was taken out of service.

They soon discovered that allowing maintenance this access to their equipment gave maintenance the chance to fix it right instead of applying Band-Aids™, as had been the previous practice. As a result, equipment uptime increased dramatically—by a factor of about four compared to prior levels of uptime. The ratio between scheduled downtime and increased run uptime was about one to three. That is, for every hour of scheduled downtime, they realized a three-hour increase in equipment uptime, the increase in uptime resulting from the virtual elimination of unscheduled downtime. Unscheduled downtime was minor in nature.

As a result, productive capacity increased dramatically. The increase in capacity allowed Production the luxury of scheduling even more downtime which in turn allowed maintenance to improve equipment performance even more. Unscheduled downtime decreased even more, and so on.

The other facilities implemented their maintenance systems but continued their former practices. They viewed the maintenance system as a way to assist maintenance, not as a way to improve on overall plant performance levels.

How is XYZ doing? Compared to their sister plants:

They outproduce all the other plants by varying margins—not bad, considering they are the smallest of the group and have the fewest production capabilities.

Their production costs are dramatically lower.

Their maintenance costs are significantly lower.

They experience fewer missed shipments—none.

They maintain lower intermediate and finished goods inventory levels.

They are capable of turning around customer orders in at least half of the time it takes the other plants to respond to similar orders.

They operate in a consistent, repeatable manner.

They operate as a team, with everyone in the facility working toward common goals.

They are able to maintain finished qoods quality levels that cannot be matched by the other plants.

They continually seek new ways to improve the skill levels of all facility employees.

Overall, they are doing well. During discussions with representatives from several of the plants, the differences between the facilities became painfully clear. XYZ continued to seek new ways to improve and to build on past accomplishments. XYZ personnel were like steamrollers; when problems arose they continued to move forward, removing all obstacles. They did not expect perfection; they expected continual improvement.

Without exception, the other facilities continued to complain about why they were not able to do things. They were still struggling with the same problems and issues that existed before they implemented their maintenance systems. When confronted with the accomplishments of the XYZ facility, all they could do is shake their heads and remark that that was not how they did things in their facilities.

The difference was clear. Management, by promoting change and by being willing to challenge the status quo, made the difference.

Rethinking the Present...
Discovering the Future:
Killark Electric

Killark Electric typifies many response-managed principles. They reinvented themselves in order to rediscover their future. For Killark, being very good was not enough; they knew they were capable of more.

Killark Electric manufactures industrial lighting fixtures, fittings, controls, enclosures, and distribution equipment primarily for hostile environments. Killark is a division of Hubbell, Inc., located in St. Louis, Missouri. A well established company, Killark has been in business for 80 years. Their product line consists of approximately 8000 distinct end items. Manufacturing is primarily configured to order. At the same time, they do manufacture a limited, though ever increasing, amount of special-order, one-of-a-kind products.

In 1988, Killark management decided to change direction to clearly distinguish themselves from their competition. Their goal was to initiate a process improvement program that would allow all departments to increase their ability to respond to evolving customer and market needs. (Within their industry they have traditionally been recognized as the service leader.) Their subsequent actions are a study in excellence. The results of their efforts allowed them not only to endure during the weak economy of the late 1980s into the early 1990s, but also to prosper during these difficult times.

Killark is driven by a desire to service their customers and to be recognized as *the* response leader within their industry. Their corporate objective is "to provide focused product offerings and to deliver them better than anyone else." Their historical ability to deliver on their objectives has allowed them to attain a position in which they are recognized as among the top three suppliers to the specialty lighting industry and one of the top two suppliers in their other markets. This achievement comes in markets that are very competitive.

In pursuit of their goals, Killark management adopted an improvement strategy that involved:

- Expanding the knowledge base of employees throughout the organization.
- Using their "new" knowledge to reexamine existing methods and practices.
- Reengineering existing processes to achieve improved levels of capability, productivity, and quality.
- Developing new marketing strategies based on their improved ability to respond.

Prior to their transformation to a world-class response-managed organization, Killark typified the traditional management and manufacturing practices that pervade much of American industry. Management and labor maintained a mutually hostile attitude and mistrust. Labor was represented by several unions, among whom there was also a feeling of mistrust.

Manufacturing was traditionally batch-oriented, producing products in large lot sizes. Production activities were organized into three primary groups: manufacture of components, painting operations, and assembly and test operations. Raw materials were either purchased or supplied by sister plants. Many purchased components were processed through numerous machining operations, then painted and finally assembled with other purchased components into final products.

Manufacturing processes were highly engineered. Final assembly operations were designed to support the batch manufacture of end items in an assembly line configuration. Shop floor labor was not encouraged to participate in any activities other than their immediate jobs. The expression of ideas or suggestions was discouraged. Typically, shop floor labor did not speak when supervisors were present. The concept of employee involvement was foreign to them. No employee would think it appropriate to contradict or to suggest improvement to any action requested by a supervisor. Creativity had been successfully eliminated from day-to-day shop floor operations. Rote response was the generally accepted rule.

Material handling was also traditional. There was lots of raw material around, stored at several facilities. A main warehouse storage facility was several miles away from the manufacturing site. In addition, many components and subassemblies were stored on several floors within the manufacturing site.

Once a production schedule had been established, the shop floor supervisors acquired the components necessary to support the schedule and literally piled them up next to the final assembly lines. Stockouts were common and often interrupted work in progress.

Manufacturing lead times required to respond to customer orders were typical for their industry, about four to six weeks.

As a result of their efforts, they have realized benefits in all areas of the company. Benefits tend to have a cascade effect, in which one benefit or improvement leads to others, and so on. The following are a *few* of the benefits realized by adopting a response-managed strategy:

Ability to Reduce Customer Response Lead Time.   Their improvements in manufacturing have allowed Killark to reduce order lead time from industry average times of four to six weeks to new response-managed times of 24 hours for standard stock items and five days or less for custom configurations.

Killark is now advertising their ability to respond. They call their program QRP for *quick-response program*. Their advertising tag line is, "Quick Response from Killark helps keep you on schedule." Their ability to respond is now a benefit that can be passed on to their customers to allow them, in turn, to be more successful.

Starting from a position of recognition as the industry leader in providing service to their customers, they are now providing levels of service that are unrivaled in their marketplace.

Team Work.   Most functions were reorganized to perform as teams. New product design teams were established, along with manufacturing teams, process improvement teams, quality improvement teams, problem-solving teams, and others. This team development recognized the interdependent nature of most business activities. They tore down the silo walls and created cross-functional teams to achieve cross-functional results.

All functions were able to benefit from this change. A typical example is in how they approached new product design. New products are created by a design team that includes representatives from Purchasing, Marketing and Sales, Manufacturing, Materials, Engineering, and in many instances vendors.

In general, the team approach has reduced the time required to achieve results and improved results. Fewer changes are made after decisions are reached, and all departments better understand how they affect their peers throughout the organization.

Improved Product Quality.   Since Killark's products are used in hostile environments, product quality is imperative. Prior to their adoption of response-managed techniques, quality was, by any standard, excellent. They perform 100-percent inspection of finished goods, with reject rates traditionally around 1.9 percent.

As a result of employee involvement activities, combined with daily problem-solving meetings held after daily production goals have been attained, they have virtually eliminated product rejects at inspection.

Improved Employee Involvement.   Employees are now involved in all aspects of manufacturing, including designing line configurations. Employees actively pursue the quality improvement of product design, components, manufacturing processes, workstation layout, and tool selection. Employees assist in determining quality problems and eliminating problem causes. Employee morale has increased dramatically. Productivity is up, quality is up, and participation is up. Management is concerned about their ability to keep pace with the level of suggestions generated by employees. The goal of management is to provide quick response to all suggestions. *People now feel that they are part of the solution–that their opinions are valued and sought after.*

Transformation of All Assembly Operations into Cells or Lines. Employees have been involved in the redesign of all assembly operations into efficient work cells or lines. Many different configurations have resulted from their efforts. There are cells, lines, U-shapes, circles, and so forth. Each area has been optimized for the products being manufactured. Manufacturing process design is based on achieving a balanced, pull product flow process configuration.

The redesign of manufacturing operations has been one of the most important steps taken to improve the ability to respond. As a result of their process redesign efforts, cycle time has been reduced and problem solving has improved. Also improved are quality, employee participation, productivity, sales, and profits.

Reliable Production Scheduling. As a result of their manufacturing process redesign efforts, they have achieved a level of performance in which productivity is reliable, repeatable, and consistent. They know how much of a specific product they can produce in a given time. When changes occur, they are positive, reflecting an increase in capability for line personnel.

The manufacturing reliability they now enjoy has allowed them to realize other benefits, such as the following.

Ability to Build to Customer Order Instead of to Forecast. As a result of their new manufacturing capability, they have been able to eliminate the need to rely on subassemblies as their only means of assembling a product in a reasonable time frame. They now invest their valuable labor and material resources only to make end items; they no longer produce and inventory subassemblies.

This capability has further allowed them to drive manufacturing directly with customer orders instead of from a forecast. As a result, they are able to quickly produce just what customers want, instead of what their forecasting system suggests they will want.

This improved capability is the foundation of their Quick-Response Program for lighting fixtures.

Reduced WIP Inventory.   Once they were able to cease producing and storing subassemblies, they realized a significant drop in the amount of WIP inventory. They estimate that they reduced WIP by more than 50 percent.

Ability to Convert Subassembly Storage Space to Raw Material Storage Space.   Once they ceased producing subassemblies, they no longer needed storage space for them. This made a considerable amount of space available for other uses. The redesign of their manufacturing processes also resulted in a more effective use of space and freed up further space. They used this new-found space to their advantage. Raw materials, which had been previously stored at a geographically remote warehouse facility, were now moved next to the assembly lines that consumed this material.

Reduced Material Handling and Associated Indirect Costs.   With raw materials now located immediately next to the production lines, material handling costs have been dramatically reduced. Instead of having to transport materials between geographically separated buildings, they now only have to move that same material a few feet to deliver it to the point of need.

The close proximity of stores to lines also allows smaller material supply lot sizes. The smaller lot sizes eliminate the need for expensive material handling equipment. In addition, the overall cost of material handling has been dramatically reduced.

Improved Material Management.   Yet another benefit of the proximity of raw and component materials was a significant improvement in material management. Prior to the move, it was very difficult to maintain accurate or timely inventory counts, consequently experiencing frequent stockouts which had considerable impact on their ability to perform to schedule. Production runs were continually being interrupted due to material shortages. One way they attempted to deal with this situation was to invest precious labor resources to produce subassemblies, hoping that this would mitigate the stockout situation. The consolidation of inventory, combined with elimination of subassembly production and with improved material handling and control, resulted in a virtual elimination of stockout situations.

Components Direct Shipped to Manufacturing. Consolidation of stores also allowed them to ship many components directly to the point of need—to the relevant manufacturing process—to meet scheduled production. This was a dramatic change. Instead of identifying a receiving dock at a remote storage facility as the delivery point for materials, they specified the manufacturing line scheduled to use the material as the delivery point. This action greatly reduced or eliminated material handling, helped them plan better, allowed for improved material management, and all but eliminated the need to store and manage many raw and component items.

Improved Supplier Relations. Direct shipping also allowed them to develop improved relationships with their suppliers. Orders were more reliable, being based more on real need instead of forecast. Lot size requirements were negotiated to reflect stable manufacturing requirements. There were fewer emergency situations previously caused by stockouts. Suppliers were now viewed as business partners instead of as adversaries. In time, they expanded their supplier relationships to achieve additional benefits in their product design efforts.

Reduced Engineering Development Cycle. The formation of product development teams was expanded to embrace new product tooling design. As a result of this transformation, design time—from engineering drawing to the tooling being ready to make parts—was reduced from four-six months to three-four months.

Killark, while being pleased with their achievements to date, still feels that they have a "long way to go" toward reaching their goals.

Their journey toward becoming a fully developed response-managed organization is not yet complete. They continue to improve and to seek further ways to enhance their ability to respond. How did they start on their journey?

The Transformation Process

For Killark, the journey began with a feeling on the part of Operations management that they could do better. They were becoming aware that other, unrelated companies were improving on current standards and began to question their ability to do the same.

The next step in the journey was to learn their possibilities. What were others doing? How well did they do it? What went well? What were the pitfalls? Members of the Operations and Engineering departments began to attend seminars and lectures, and to seek out reading materials on the so-called "world-class methods."

This is how I first met the folks from Killark. They attended a just-in-time manufacturing seminar I was presenting for the Washington University CIM Center. As they acquired an understanding of what was happening in the world-class arena, they soon realized that their best approach would be to seek outside assistance to aid them in transforming their company into a response-managed organization. From the beginning, they were able to realize the end purpose of the many programs currently in vogue: response.

They next hired an outside consulting firm, Steve Levit Associates, to assist them in developing a transformation strategy and in successfully implementing that strategy. Working with the consultants, they set out to identify which of their existing activities would best serve as a starting place. The primary criterion in selecting their demonstration area was its ability to be successful in achieving the objectives to be established for the project. For our transformation process we selected the assembly operations associated with a family of lighting products.

Once they determined where they would start the transformation process (the product area), they were able to form a transformation team. The team was composed of several shop floor people who were currently involved in the manufacture of the selected product line, a representative from Manufacturing Engineering, their materials manager, the Operations manager, the shop floor supervisor who was currently supervising the line selected for the transformation process, and a representative from Purchasing. The transformation team would ultimately be responsible for redesigning the existing manufacturing process to transform it into the desired response-managed process.

The next step in the transformation process was to involve everyone in the facility in the process. This level of involvement was considered crucial to the long-term success of their undertaking. The intent was to prevent rumors from starting. It was also to establish an environment in which people would feel that their input was desired and would understand what was about to happen, why it was happening, what it would mean to them, and what it would mean to the corporation.

To involve all personnel, a series of presentations was scheduled. Each presentation was limited in attendance to ensure participation and open dialogue. We found that an audience size of 50 to 60 was about as large as we could go and still achieve our presentation goals. During these meetings, plant personnel had the opportunity to meet transformation team members, as well as the management personnel participating in the process.

One important goal for these sessions was to establish new expectations. We were attempting to significantly change the direction of the corporation with regard to employee-employer relations. It was important to let people know that the intent of this program was not to find new ways to eliminate their jobs.

After we completed the education phase, the Project Team began the task of documenting how they currently built the products associated with the transformation line. The existing process of manufacture was documented. Documentation included both the analysis of material movements and operations, as well as the inclusion of details covering existing methods and procedures.

Concurrent with their documentation activities, the team began to develop a project charter, which detailed their goals, how they were going to achieve the goals, who would be involved in achieving the goals, and what their responsibilities would be. They also listed the benefits they expected to realize when they achieved their goals and an outline of how they were going to plan and manage the transformation process.

Once the team completed their process documentation tasks, they considered ways to reengineer the existing process to transform it into a response-managed process. We decided to adopt just-in-time manufacturing principles as the basis for our transformation in manufacturing.

The documentation activity uncovered many interesting facts:

- Under current rules, the products and materials associated with the transformation line traveled over one mile during the manufacturing process. This distance did not include the distance between storage facilities or between floors in the manufacturing facility.

- Subassemblies were stored in several places throughout the facility. It was possible for some units of a subassembly to be on an elevator, in transit to one of the storage areas, while other units of the same subassembly were on the elevator to be delivered to manufacturing to complete a customer order. The subassemblies being sent to storage came from the same place as the subassemblies just pulled from storage were going to. They were each on the same elevator at the same time.

- The large number of partially built units and the number of planned subassemblies took up so much floor space that a separate building was required to store raw materials.

- Because raw materials were stored at a geographically separated site, material control was difficult. As a result, stockouts were occurring all too frequently.

- Manufacturing cycle time was equal to industry standards of several weeks.

Among our reengineering goals were a desire to reduce space, eliminate the need to store subassemblies, build only finished goods (not partially build anything), move raw materials to the manufacturing facility, improve quality, and improve productivity and manufacturing efficiency.

During the reengineering process, the transformation team had to confront several special problems. First—shop floor personnel were not used to expressing opinions in the presence of supervision. If our process was to work, it was vital for these same people to become vocal and to contribute. We spent the first few team meetings just trying to overcome this obstacle and to encourage people to speak openly.

Note: This situation is all too common. In many traditional environments, shop floor personnel have learned that it is not appropriate for them to express opinions or to speak openly in the presence of management. Management is anyone above them. This situation poses several distinct problems:

- The people who are not talking are often the same people who possess the knowledge necessary to successfully reengineer a process.

- One element of success is honesty. Reengineering should be based on accurate information about current process and procedure. Honest feedback is hampered when those who should be providing the feedback will not speak openly for fear of reprisal.

- Ongoing dialogue is a necessary element of any improvement program. This dialogue will not take place unless fear or reprisal can be overcome.

- Teamwork requires mutual participation. Mutual participation requires mutual understanding of the issues pertaining to the team and buying in to the approaches adopted by the team. None of this is possible without open communication among all team members.

This situation has existed in virtually every cross-functional team situation I have ever encountered. Once this hurdle is overcome, teams become vibrant and alive, capable of achieving previously unheard of levels of performance.

Our next special problem was related to the large number of distinct end items that could be produced on the transformation line. Each end item required different components. How could we manage this diversity? The solution to this problem occurred when we were able to overcome the communication issue. We were discussing this problem during one of our first meetings when one of the shop floor people raised her hand. This was a timid gesture; she was uncertain, yet bold, in chancing to speak. She thought that she could see a way to solve the problem of product diversity. She was about to offer a way to manage the different component mix possibilities, allowing the line to build any end item for which it was designed in any quantity. Speaking softly and glancing around nervously, she offered a truly elegant solution to a significant problem.

While the rest of us could not see the forest for the trees, she was not only able to see the forest but saw a path through it. Her solution was simple in design, economical to execute, and elegant in its ability to allow the line to produce individual products easily without confusion.

Our last special problem was also a common one: "This is how we have always done it," or *the inability to see beyond yesterday.* There were some specific challenges in this area. Once the team became comfortable with the notion that tomorrow can indeed be different from yesterday, they were able to suggest and eventually adapt several breakthrough solutions to basic manufacturing problems. These breakthroughs allowed them to achieve the levels of response that they are capable of today. (I am being deliberately vague as to the specific nature of these breakthroughs to protect Killark's competitive advantage.)

Once the team suggested how the line should be set up to achieve our goals, the engineering team began the process of setting up the new line. While they were doing this, the team continued its activities and began to develop new procedures and policies by which to manage the new response-managed line.

We then found that what works in one situation may not work in other similar ones. A good example of this was our intention to use a production control board to publish daily production schedules and to report daily progress against these schedules. The team thought this would be a good idea, but the manufacturing line staff did not, even though many of the line staff had been on the transformation team. As a result the production control board approach was dropped. In its place the line retained a production scheduling system similar to the one that existed prior to the establishment of the transformation line.

Our approach to end-of-day team meetings, to be held once daily production goals had been achieved, was first adopted, then dropped when the meetings were felt to be productive no longer. We could not have predicted this outcome when we began the project. Initially, shop floor personnel were excited by the prospect of "finishing" during the day and of having meetings. The meetings were very productive and contributed to solving virtually all the recurring problems confronting Manufacturing. However, once most problems had been solved, shop floor personnel became impatient with the meetings and voted to skip the meetings. Instead of meeting, they decided to continue to produce product.

This was a very new development—line personnel voting to increase productivity instead of seeking ways to avoid work.

The new line was a smashing success for all concerned. By any measure their efforts to transform existing operations to achieve response-managed performance levels was a success. As a result of their initial success, they were able to work off their excess inventory of subassemblies and partially completed assemblies. This freed-up space could be used to better advantage. They were able to move component parts inventory from their remote warehouse into the new available space. This action reduced stockouts, which improved efficiency, which improved productivity, which lowered operating costs, and so forth.

They began to migrate their initial success to other product lines. Within several months, they were able to convert all remaining manufacturing assembly operations to response-managed lines, or cells, or U-shapes, or Ls, to whatever configuration was most appropriate for the product or products to be produced there.

Each transformation yielded results similar to their initial transformation line.

One more challenge remained—to begin using their new level of capability as a competitive weapon. To achieve this, Manufacturing had to convince Sales that something different and wonderful had happened. Sales had to believe that they now had something to sell that was unmatched by any of their competitors—they could respond!

Over time (it was several months before a salesman took advantage of this new capability and booked an order based on their ability to respond), Killark took a proactive approach toward their new ability to respond and they began to advertise it both internally to other departments and functions, as well as externally. They developed their quick-response program aptly named QRP.

They also began to inform sales personnel of their new capabilities and presented success stories in their internal sales newsletter *REP RAP*. They began to advertise to Sales.

Killark now feels that they have created a firm foundation on which to base their future. (See The *REP RAP* newsletter samples on the following pages.)

QRP for lighting provides accelerated delivery of the Hazardous and Hostile Location fixtures you need most.

Standard stock fixtures selected from the PICK LIST will be shipped from the factory **within 24 hours.** EZ and VM Series Stock fixtures are supplied with multi-tap (120, 208, 240, 277 volt) ballasts.

Custom configured fixtures found on the PICK LIST will be shipped from the factory **in 5 days or less.** EZ and VM Series custom configurations include 480 volt ballasts and the following options:

BP	Ballast Protector "EZ"/"VM" Series
IR	Instant Restrike "VM" Series
R	Instant Restrike "EZ" Series
QTZ	Auxiliary Quartz "VM" Series
Q	Auxiliary Quartz "EZ" Series

Note: Please specify QRP service at time of order placement. Delivery time may vary according to quantities ordered.

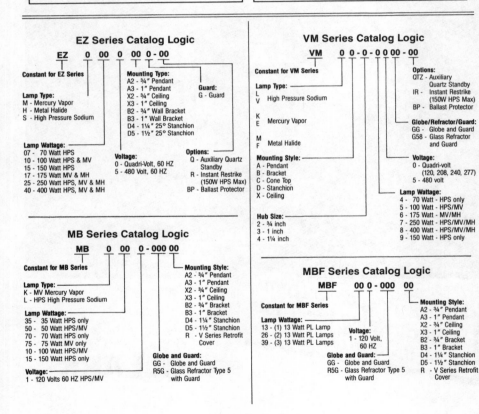

PICK LIST

HOSTILE-LITE™ EZ Series
MOGUL BASE
H.I.D. LUMINAIRES
CLASS I, DIVISIONS 1 & 2, GROUPS C & D
CLASS II, DIVISIONS 1 & 2, GROUPS E,F & G —
CLASS III, DIVISIONS 1 & 2
NEMA 3,4,4X,7CD,9EFG

EZ Series — HPS
Stock	Custom
EZS070A2G	EZS075A2G
EZS070A3G	EZS075A3G
EZS070B2G	EZS075B2G
EZS070B3G	EZS075B3G
EZS070D4G	EZS075D4G
EZS070D5G	EZS075D5G
EZS070X2G	EZS075X2G
EZS070X3G	EZS075X3G
EZS100A2G	EZS105A2G
EZS100A3G	EZS105A3G
EZS100B2G	EZS105B2G
EZS100B3G	EZS105B3G
EZS100D4G	EZS105D4G
EZS100D5G	EZS105D5G
EZS100X2G	EZS105X2G
EZS100X3G	EZS105X3G
EZS150A2G	EZS155A2G
EZS150A3G	EZS155A3G
EZS150B2G	EZS155B2G
EZS150B3G	EZS155B3G
EZS150D4G	EZS155D4G
EZS150D5G	EZS155D5G
EZS150X2G	EZS155X2G
EZS150X3G	EZS155X3G
EZS250A2G	EZS255A2G
EZS250A3G	EZS255A3G
EZS250B2G	EZS255B2G
EZS250B3G	EZS255B3G
EZS250D4G	EZS255D4G
EZS250D5G	EZS255D5G
EZS250X2G	EZS255X2G
EZS250X3G	EZS255X3G
EZS400A2G	EZS405A2G
EZS400A3G	EZS405A3G
EZS400B2G	EZS405B2G
EZS400B3G	EZS405B3G
EZS400D4G	EZS405D4G
EZS400D5G	EZS405D5G
EZS400X2G	EZS405X2G
EZS400X3G	EZS405X3G

EZ Series - MH
Stock	Custom
EZH170A2G	EZH175A2G
EZH170A3G	EZH175A3G
EZH170B2G	EZH175B2G
EZH170B3G	EZH175B3G
EZH170D4G	EZH175D4G
EZH170D5G	EZH175D5G
EZH170X2G	EZH175X2G
EZH170X3G	EZH175X3G
EZH250A2G	EZH255A2G
EZH250A3G	EZH255A3G
EZH250B2G	EZH255B2G
EZH250B3G	EZH255B3G
EZH250D4G	EZH255D4G
EZH250D5G	EZH255D5G
EZH250X2G	EZH255X2G
EZH250X3G	EZH255X3G
EZH400A2G	EZH405A2G
EZH400A3G	EZH405A3G
EZH400B2G	EZH405B2G
EZH400B3G	EZH405B3G
EZH400D4G	EZH405D4G
EZH400D5G	EZH405D5G
EZH400X2G	EZH405X2G
EZH400X3G	EZH405X3G

EZ Series - MV
Stock	Custom
EZM100A2G	EZM105A2G
EZM100A3G	EZM105A3G
EZM100B2G	EZM105B2G
EZM100B3G	EZM105B3G
EZM100D4G	EZM105D4G
EZM100D5G	EZM105D5G
EZM100X2G	EZM105X2G
EZM100X3G	EZM105X3G
EZM170A2G	EZM175A2G
EZM170A3G	EZM175A3G
EZM170B2G	EZM175B2G
EZM170B3G	EZM175B3G
EZM170D4G	EZM175D4G
EZM170D5G	EZM175D5G
EZM170X2G	EZM175X2G
EZM170X3G	EZM175X3G
EZM250A2G	EZM255A2G
EZM250A3G	EZM255A3G
EZM250B2G	EZM255B2G
EZM250B3G	EZM255B3G
EZM250D4G	EZM255D4G
EZM250D5G	EZM255D5G
EZM250X2G	EZM255X2G
EZM250X3G	EZM255X3G
EZM400A2G	EZM405A2G
EZM400A3G	EZM405A3G
EZM400B2G	EZM405B2G
EZM400B3G	EZM405B3G
EZM400D4G	EZM405D4G
EZM400D5G	EZM405D5G
EZM400X2G	EZM405X2G
EZM400X3G	EZM405X3G

CERTI-LITE® VM Series
MOGUL BASE
H.I.D. LUMINAIRES
CLASS I, DIVISION 2, GROUPS A,B,C,D
CLASS II, DIVISIONS 1 & 2, GROUPS E,F & G —
CLASS III, DIVISIONS 1 & 2
NEMA 3,4,4X,9EFG

VM Series - HPS
Stock	Custom
VMLA-2-40G58	VMLA-2-45G58
VMLA-2-40GG	VMLA-2-45GG
VMLA-2-50G58	VMLA-2-55G58
VMLA-2-50GG	VMLA-2-55GG
VMLA-2-90G58	VMLA-2-95G58
VMLA-2-90GG	VMLA-2-95GG
VMLB-2-40G58	VMLB-2-45G58
VMLB-2-40GG	VMLB-2-45GG
VMLB-2-50G58	VMLB-2-55G58
VMLB-2-50GG	VMLB-2-55GG
VMLB-2-90G58	VMLB-2-95G58
VMLB-2-90GG	VMLB-2-95GG
VMLC-2-40G58	VMLC-2-45G58
VMLC-2-40GG	VMLC-2-45GG
VMLC-2-50G58	VMLC-2-55G58
VMLC-2-50GG	VMLC-2-55GG
VMLC-2-90G58	VMLC-2-95G58
VMLC-2-90GG	VMLC-2-95GG
VMLD-4-40G58	VMLD-4-45G58
VMLD-4-40GG	VMLD-4-45GG
VMLD-4-50G58	VMLD-4-55G58
VMLD-4-50GG	VMLD-4-55GG
VMLD-4-90G58	VMLD-4-95G58
VMLD-4-90GG	VMLD-4-95GG
VMLX-2-40G58	VMLX-2-45G58
VMLX-2-40GG	VMLX-2-45GG
VMLX-2-50G58	VMLX-2-55G58
VMLX-2-50GG	VMLX-2-55GG
VMLX-2-90G58	VMLX-2-95G58
VMLX-2-90GG	VMLX-2-95GG

VM Series - HPS
Stock	Custom
VMVA-2-70G5	VMVA-2-75G5
VMVA-2-70GG	VMVA-2-75GG
VMVA-2-80G5	VMVA-2-85G5
VMVA-2-80GG	VMVA-2-85GG
VMVB-2-70G5	VMVB-2-75G5
VMVB-2-70GG	VMVB-2-75GG
VMVB-2-80G5	VMVB-2-85G5
VMVB-2-80GG	VMVB-2-85GG
VMVC-2-70G5	VMVC-2-75G5
VMVC-2-70GG	VMVC-2-75GG
VMVC-2-80G5	VMVC-2-85G5
VMVC 2-80GG	VMVC-2-85GG
VMVD-4-70G5	VMVD-4-75G5
VMVD-4-70GG	VMVD-4-75GG
VMVD-4-80G5	VMVD-4-85G5
VMVD-4-80GG	VMVD-4-85GG
VMVX-2-70G5	VMVX-2-75G5
VMVX-2-70GG	VMVX-2-75GG
VMVX-2-80G5	VMVX-2-85G5
VMVX-2-80GG	VMVX-2-85GG

VM Series - MH
Stock	Custom
VMMA-2-60G58	VMMA-2-65G58
VMMA-2-60GG	VMMA-2-65GG
VMMA-2-70G58	VMMA-2-75G58
VMMA-2-70GG	VMMA-2-75GG
VMMB-2-60G58	VMMB-2-65G58
VMMB-2-60GG	VMMB-2-65GG
VMMB-2-70G58	VMMB-2-75G58
VMMB-2-70GG	VMMB-2-75GG
VMMC-2-60G58	VMMC-2-65G58
VMMC-2-60GG	VMMC-2-65GG
VMMC-2-70G58	VMMC-2-75G58
VMMC-2-70GG	VMMC-2-75GG
VMMD-4-60G58	VMMD-4-65G58
VMMD-4-60GG	VMMD-4-65GG
VMMD-4-70G58	VMMD-4-75G58
VMMD-4-70GG	VMMD-4-75GG
VMMX-2-60G58	VMMX-2-65G58
VMMX-2-60GG	VMMX-2-65GG
VMMX-2-70G58	VMMX-2-75G58
VMMX-2-70GG	VMMX-2-75GG
VMFA-2-80G5	VMFA-2-85G5
VMFA-2-80GG	VMFA-2-85GG
VMFB-2-80G5	VMFB-2-85G5
VMFB-2-80GG	VMFB-2-85GG
VMFC-2-80G5	VMFC-2-85G5
VMFC-2-80GG	VMFC-2-85GG
VMFD-4-80G5	VMFD-4-85G5
VMFD-4-80GG	VMFD-4-85GG
VMFX-2-80G5	VMFX-2-85G5
VMFX-2-80GG	VMFX-2-85GG

VM Series - MV
Stock	Custom
VMKA-2-50G58	VMKA-2-55G58
VMKA-2-50GG	VMKA-2-55GG
VMKA-2-60G58	VMKA-2-65G58
VMKA-2-60GG	VMKA-2-65GG
VMKA-2-70G58	VMKA-2-75G58
VMKA-2-70GG	VMKA-2-75GG
VMKB-2-50G58	VMKB-2-55G58
VMKB-2-50GG	VMKB-2-55GG
VMKB-2-60G58	VMKB-2-65G58
VMKB-2-60GG	VMKB-2-65GG
VMKB-2-70G58	VMKB-2-75G58
VMKB-2-70GG	VMKB-2-75GG

PICK LIST

VM Series — MV

Stock	Custom
VMKC-2-50G58	VMKC-2-55G58
VMKC-2-50GG	VMKC-2-55GG
VMKC-2-60G58	VMKC-2-65G58
VMKC-2-60GG	VMKC-2-65GG
VMKC-2-70G58	VMKC-2-75G58
VMKC-2-70GG	VMKC-2-75GG
VMKD-4-50G58	VMKD-4-55G58
VMKD-4-50GG	VMKD-4-55GG
VMKD-4-60G58	VMKD-4-65G58
VMKD-4-60GG	VMKD-4-65GG
VMKD-4-70G58	VMKD-4-75G58
VMKD-4-70GG	VMKD-4-75GG
VMKX-2-50G58	VMKX-2-55G58
VMKX-2-50GG	VMKX-2-55GG
VMKX-2-60G58	VMKX-2-65G58
VMKX-2-60GG	VMKX-2-65GG
VMKX-2-70G58	VMKX-2-75G58
VMKX-2-70GG	VMKX-2-75GG
VMEA-2-80G5	VMEA-2-85G5
VMEA-2-80GG	VMEA-2-85GG
VMEB-2-80G5	VMEB-2-85G5
VMEB-2-80GG	VMEB-2-85GG
VMEC-2-80G5	VMEC-2-85G5
VMEC-2-80GG	VMEC-2-85GG
VMED-4-80G5	VMED-4-85G5
VMED-4-80GG	VMED-4-85GG
VMEX-2-80G5	VMEX-2-85G5
VMEX-2-80GG	VMEX-2-85GG

CERTI-LITE®
MB Series
MEDIUM BASE
HIGH PRESSURE SODIUM
H.I.D. LUMINAIRES

CLASS I, DIVISION 2, GROUPS A,B,C & D
CLASS II, DIVISIONS 1 & 2, GROUPS E,F & G —
CLASS III, DIVISIONS 1 & 2
NEMA 3,4,4X,9EFG

MB Series - HPS

Stock	Custom
MBL501-GGA2	MBL351-GGA2
MBL501-GGA3	MBL351-GGA3
MBL501-GGB2	MBL351-GGB2
MBL501-GGB3	MBL351-GGB3
MBL501-GGD4	MBL351-GGD4
MBL501-GGD5	MBL351-GGD5
MBL501-GGR	MBL351-GGR
MBL501-GGX2	MBL351-GGX2
MBL501-GGX3	MBL351-GGX3
MBL501-R5GA2	MBL351-R5GA2
MBL501-R5GA3	MBL351-R5GA3
MBL501-R5GB2	MBL351-R5GB2
MBL501-R5GB3	MBL351-R5GB3
MBL501-R5GD4	MBL351-R5GD4
MBL501-R5GD5	MBL351-R5GD5
MBL501-R5GR	MBL351-R5GR
MBL501-R5GX2	MBL351-R5GX2
MBL501-R5GX3	MBL351-R5GX3

MB Series - HPS

Stock	Stock
MBL701-GGA2	MBL101-R5GA2
MBL701-GGA3	MBL101-R5GA3
MBL701-GGB2	MBL101-R5GB2
MBL701-GGB3	MBL101-R5GB3
MBL701-GGD4	MBL101-R5GD4
MBL701-GGD5	MBL101-R5GD5
MBL701-GGR	MBL101-R5GR
MBL701-GGX2	MBL101-R5GX2
MBL701-GGX3	MBL101-R5GX3
MBL701-R5GA2	
MBL701-R5GA3	MBL151-GGA2
MBL701-R5GB2	MBL151-GGA3
MBL701-R5GB3	MBL151-GGB2
MBL701-R5GD4	MBL151-GGB3
MBL701-R5GD5	MBL151-GGD4
MBL701-R5GR	MBL151-GGD5
MBL701-R5GX2	MBL151-GGR
MBL701-R5GX3	MBL151-GGX3
	MBL151-R5GA2
MBL101-GGA2	MBL151-R5GA3
MBL101-GGA3	MBL151-R5GB2
MBL101-GGB2	MBL151-R5GB3
MBL101-GGB3	MBL151-R5GD4
MBL101-GGD4	MBL151-R5GD5
MBL101-GGD5	MBL151-R5GR
MBL101-GGR	MBL151-R5GX2
MBL101-GGX2	MBL151-R5GX3
MBL101-GGX3	

MB Series - MV

Stock	Stock
MBK101-GGA2	MBK751-GGA2
MBK101-GGA3	MBK751-GGA3
MBK101-GGB2	MBK751-GGB2
MBK101-GGB3	MBK751-GGB3
MBK101-GGD4	MBK751-GGD4
MBK101-GGD5	MBK751-GGD5
MBK101-GGR	MBK751-GGR
MBK101-GGX2	MBK751-GGX2
MBK101-GGX3	MBK751-GGX3
MBK101-R5GA2	MBK751-R5GA2
MBK101-R5GA3	MBK751-R5GA3
MBK101-R5GB2	MBK751-R5GB2
MBK101-R5GB3	MBK751-R5GB3
MBK101-R5GD4	MBK751-R5GD4
MBK101-R5GD5	MBK751-R5GD5
MBK101-R5GR	MBK751-R5GR
MBK101-R5GX2	MBK751-R5GX2
MBK101-R5GX3	MBK751-R5GX3

MB Series - MV

Custom	Custom
MBK501-GGA2	MBK501-R5GA2
MBK501-GGA3	MBK501-R5GA3
MBK501-GGB2	MBK501-R5GB2
MBK501-GGB3	MBK501-R5GB3
MBK501-GGD4	MBK501-R5GD4
MBK501-GGD5	MBK501-R5GD5
MBK501-GGR	MBK501-R5GR
MBK501-GGX2	MBK501-R5GX2
MBK501-GGX3	MBK501-R5BX3

CERTI-LITE®
MBF Series
BI-PIN PL
FLUORESCENT LUMINAIRES

CLASS I, DIVISION 2, GROUPS A,B,C & D
CLASS II, DIVISIONS 1 & 2, GROUPS E,F & G —
CLASS III, DIVISIONS 1 & 2
NEMA 3,4,4X,9EFG

MBF Series - Fluorescent

Stock	Stock
MBF131-GGA2	MBF261-GGA2
MBF131-GGA3	MBF261-GGA3
MBF131-GGB2	MBF261-GGB2
MBF131-GGB3	MBF261-GGD4
MBF131-GGD5	MBF261-GGD5
MBF131-GGR	MBF261-GGR
MBF131-GGX2	MBF261-GGX2
MBF131-GGX3	MBF261-GGX3
MBF131-R5GA2	MBF261-R5GA2
MBF131-R5GA3	MBF261-R5GA3
MBF131-R5GB2	MBF261-R5GB2
MBF131-R5GB3	MBF261-R5GB3
MBF131-R5GD4	MBF261-R5GD4
MBF131-R5GD5	MBF261-R5GD5
MBF131-R5GR	MBF261-R5GR
MBF131-R5GX2	MBF261-R5GX2
MBF131-R5GX3	MBF261-R5GX3

MBF Series - Fluorescent

Custom	Custom
MBF391-GGA2	MBF391-R5GD4
MBF391-GGA3	MBF391-R5GD5
MBF391-GGB2	MBF391-R5GR
MBF391-GGB3	MBF391-R5GX2
MBF391-GGD4	MBF391-R5GX3
MBF391-GGD5	MBF391-R5GA3
MBF391-GGR	MBF391-R5GA2
MBF391-GGX2	MBF391-R5GB2
MBF391-GGX3	MBF391-R5GB3

When you need hazardous location lighting fixtures or custom enclosures **in-a-hurry**, specify QRP service from Killark.

HUBBELL • **KILLARK**

KILLARK ELECTRIC MANUFACTURING COMPANY
A Subsidiary of Hubbell Incorporated
P.O. BOX 5325 • ST. LOUIS, MISSOURI 63115-0325 • U.S.A.
Telephone (314) 531-0460 • FAX: (314) 531-7164

Copyright 1991

 **KILLARK**

REP RAP

THE NEWSLETTER FOR KILLARK SALES REPRESENTATIVES

ISSUE #39　　　　　　　　　　　　　　　　**JUNE, 1990**

BUILDING FOR SUCCESS

Previewed in last month's newsletter were some of the sales tools in development that will support the anticipated August 15th introduction of the Hostile-Lite™ EZ series fixture.

To prepare for this launch a world class manufacturing (a/k/a Just-In-Time) system for the EZ series is now being put into place at Killark.

The illustration to the left shows how the system looks. The diagram below demonstrates how the system will work.

Manufacturing Engineer Doug Richard, who recommended the "worksmart" system and is overseeing its installation, says that this modular J.I.T. assembly line is based on engineered, high-strength aluminum tubing joined by poly-carbonate fittings. Work in progress moves down the transport line, on carts, and on through electrical testing to final assembly and packaging. The carts continue to the head of the line to start the process again. A series of integrated and adjacent workstations speed assembly and part movement functions. The modular construction of the system allows new manufacturing requirements to be met easily and quickly.

What does this mean to our sales representatives and customers? Just as QRP has set new standards in the availability of custom enclosures, so too J.I.T. manufacturing will provide *LIGHT*ning fast deliveries on EZ series fixtures of both standard _and_ special configurations.

Specification Engineer Bill Earnst is also building for success **in the marketplace** by securing a fixture specification with an engineering firm involved in an overseas job.

The application is for a petrochemical plant which may require as many as **1,400** HID explosion-proof fixtures. The EZ series is specified. This opportunity demonstrates the tremendous sales potential of this new product.

Landing such an order certainly would put the new J.I.T. line through its paces.

STATION #6 — HID Testing of finished ballast tanks

STATION #5 — Wiring #2

STATION #4 — Wiring #1

STATION #3 — Sockets, internal reflectors installed

STATION #7 — Final assembly of glass globes

STATION #8 — Packing

STATION #1 — Ballast tank put on line, nameplate attached

STATION #2 — Brackets, ballast components installed

FINISH ↓

START ↑

 **KILLARK**

REP RAP

PROFIT IMPROVEMENT PROGRAM

The Killark Profit Improvement Program is the next generation of our popular and successful Distributor Support Program, which was introduced back in June of 1987.

PIP continues the DSP tradition of transaction and cost containment and enhanced customer service by removing many of the typical barriers to a meaningful business relationship. PIP goes beyond DSP in making available a whole new range of program elements designed to simplify implementation and maximize the benefits of profit enhancement.

The Profit Improvement Program unites the unique abilities of individual divisions under the strength of the Hubbell brand name. Specific PIP elements include:

- Electronic Communication
- Optimum Service
- Co-op Marketing
- Inventory Management

- Bar Coding
- Mutual Planning
- Trade Pricing
- Productivity Incentives

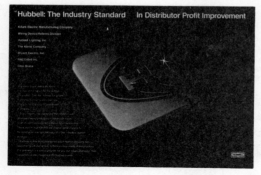

Hubbell: The Industry Standard   In Distributor Profit Improvement

CONDUCT YOUR OWN RISK FREE CORROSION CHALLENGE!

November is National Corrosion Challenge month. The Corrosion Challenge advertising insert (pictured above) appeared in the October issue of "Plant Engineering" magazine. All inquiries generated will be sent to your Regional Manager, who in turn, will assign them over to the appropriate representative for follow-up and conversion.

Of course, advertising is just one component of the Corrosion Challenge campaign. To be successful, the Corrosion Challenge must be promoted vigorously by the Killark sales force. Representatives with foresight realize that the Corrosion Challenge is an opportunity to plant the seed in 1992 at a plant with corrosion problems, and reap the benefits in 1993 and beyond. All it takes is the conversion of one plant per territory to make the program a success.

Several Killark representatives have been doing an excellent job taking advantage of the Corrosion Challenge opportunity. Notably, Lisa Cottuli in Boston, and Norm Williams in San Francisco, have been doing what it takes to make the program a success.

We are expecting each representative territory to establish a minimum of 5 Corrosion Challenge trials. Call Steve Ruane or Mac Criswell if you have any questions about the program.

Additional PIP elements, tailored to the unique needs of Killark's business environment, have been defined in PIP material previously sent to Killark Regional Managers.

Your Regional Manager has primary responsibility for directing implementation with potential program participants. He is your key contact for PIP questions you may have and support materials you would like to acquire.

Timing is very critical for the best implementation of PIP. Program presentations involving Killark sales representatives are now being made to candidate distributors.

The objective is to begin 1993 with a "clean slate" of committed key distributors and marketing action plans that reflect our mutual commitment to business growth.

Killark Electric Manufacturing Company, A Subsidiary of Hubbell Incorporated, Box 5325, St. Louis, MO 63115, 314-531-0460 FAX 314-531-7164

NEWS FROM THE

EASTERN REGION
Reg. Mgr. John Palembas

- **Rich Diego** wrote a Killark specification for Quantum® enclosures for an engineering firm who specializes in designing equipment for the pharmaceutical industry. The tightly written specification should help to keep the competition at bay and bring in a steady stream of business. Rich has also been working with distributors to create opportunities and write orders for Killark's recently introduced NVQ Series non-metallic fluorescent fixture. End-user applications include:

  - A major candy producer is using NVQ ceiling mounted fixtures with polycarbonate globes in cooling tunnels.
  - NVQ bracket mounted fixtures with ruby globes are being used by an industrial firm as long-life fire alarm, pull station lights.
  - A masonry products supplier is using NVQ bracket mounted fixtures in a plant where vibration quickly shatters filaments of incandescent lamps.

- **Eric Goldberg** made a joint call with a distributor salesman on a major producer of cookies in Philadelphia. This facility is converting to portable processing equipment that can be moved about for cleaning and repair. The plant engineer was favorably impressed with Eric's demonstration of CES Series Plugs and Receptacles. Eric stressed the non-metallic construction, suitability for wash down, and interlocking feature that prevents the plug being removed in the "ON" position. An initial order for plug and receptacle sets was written on the spot at book price. Killark had the material in stock and ready for shipment.

SOUTHEAST REGION
Reg. Mgr. Bill Colbert

- **Alex Erwin** and **Tom Gorin** worked closely with a key Killark distributor to break a competitor's hold on a local utility. For years all the lighting business has been going to a non-Killark distributor. Through Alex's and Tom's efforts, Killark was accepted as an approved supplier and a blanket order was written for Certi-Lite® VM Series fixtures. This is a handsome piece of business that has been won in large part to Alex's "never give up" attitude.

- The Southeast Region received a large order for EXB and DB Series enclosures. A mining company will use the enclosures to house controls for conveyor equipment. Killark Engineering's **Mike Schinner** provided timely technical assistance which was instrumental in securing the order.

- **Howard Clayton** recently secured an order from a large OEM for a quantity of Killark-Stahl 30.5 Series operators. Howard says that when selling the 30.5 Series of pushbuttons and selector switches, his offering is occasionally compared to those of Square D or Allen-Bradley. Both of these companies use standard location operators and hermetically sealed contact blocks for Class I, Division 2 suitability. Few distributors or large industrials stock these special contact blocks. Should an electrician unknowingly substitute a standard contact block, explosion and injury could result. Advising customers to specify Killark-Stahl 30.5 Series devices, says Howard, eliminates this possibility.

NORTH CENTRAL REGION
Reg. Mgr. Jack Kilmer

- Efforts to do business with a major steel producer in the Great Lakes Region had only been met with marginal success. But recently an opportunity arose when **Dan Carney** was called in by the Chief Engineer for a special application. The engineer required a two-speed reversible starter with anti-plugging relays in a Class I, Division 2, Group B enclosure and he needed it "yesterday". Initially, both Killark and the competition quoted a 4 week delivery. With some assistance from **Joe Laminger**, the two weeks delivery achieved allowed us to snatch the order away from competition. **Steve Dudley**, Supervisor of Control Systems, provided the engineering and made absolutely certain the starter was shipped on the promised date. This service elevates Killark to a status never before achieved at this account. We have since received a commitment to purchase 8030 Series control stations and have become their preferred supplier of NEMA 7 boxes.

- A manufacturer of liquid filter equipment seeking to broaden their penetration of the European market had little experience with international hazardous location requirements, reports **Bill Collin**. Killark-Stahl was able to provide an enclosure system to house their programmable controller, operators and terminals that would have the special certifications required. Without Killark's assistance, this user would have had to hire an outside engineer to design and specify such a system. The first order for two of these systems is pending.

KILLARK SALES TEAM

SOUTH CENTRAL REGION
Reg. Mgr. Mike Roach

- **Lee Halbur of Lesco** reports that in October, Lesco and Dunwoody Institute hosted a Fall Technical Conference. The audience of over 100 included area engineering professionals plus senior electrical students from Dunwoody. **Shane Hawk** introduced the group to Killark-Stahl products and glo-bal standards and applications. A display of products allowed hands-on inspection.

- Solve application problems where motors are used with CES Series plugs and receptacles, says **David Bean**. A petrochemical plant in Texas was experiencing long downtimes as a large drive motor had to be unwired and removed periodically to perform a particular maintenance operation. Through use of a CES Series plug and receptacle, time and labor required to disconnect and re-connect the motor was eliminated.

- **Rusty Pevehouse** and **Dave Wiltse** are seen below examining a Killark-Stahl Zone 1 panelboard. This is one of 3 that are destined for an offshore oil rig in Nigeria. Rusty and Dave coordinated with **Heinz Bockle** to write the order.

WESTERN REGION
Reg. Mgr. Bud Burton

- **John Robles of the Robert Amey Company** made a joint call with a Killark distributor on a rocket research facility. This resulted in an inquiry for a large number of explosion-proof EKJS Series stainless steel flexible couplings. While this category of fittings is sometimes overlooked, it can pay to go to "great lengths" to secure such business.

- **Dave Ispas** made joint distributor calls on two area chemical plants. After showing Killark's NVQ fixture around, both facilities have submitted inquiries for NVQ fixtures with green globes to be used above eyewash stations. This will comply with a new OSHA rule.

- **Phillip Cardin of the Stevens Sales Company** reports on the following:

  - Two 8146 Series control panels were specified by the Idaho National Engineering Lab for a hazardous waste drain line project. The contractor, who purchased and installed the panels, liked the product, price and service so well that Stevens Sales has since bid on 2 other projects. The contractor said he intends to use Killark-Stahl products for all his hazardous location control needs in the future.

  - The world's leading supplier of automotive air bags is "standardized" on Killark lighting products due to a flawless history of performance in their hazardous and corrosive sodium azide environment. To date, Stevens Sales has participated in the construction of 5 new manufacturing buildings for this client. Killark lighting, as well as fittings products, have been used extensively.

TOP SALES PERFORMERS

Congratulations to the following sales representatives who have achieved notable growth through October.

Ranking by performance for October YTD is as follows:

Representative	Terr.	Ranking
Robert Amey	MT/E WA	#1
Assoc. Sales	S. NV	#2
FRM	FL	#3
Desert Sales	NM	#4
B. Polk	Greensboro	#5
R. Diego	CT	#6
S. Lytle	N. IN	#7
D. Carney	Detroit	#8
Robert Amey	W. WA	#9
Bar Elec.	AK	#10
Stevens Sales	UT	#11
D. Rak	S. IN	#12
J.D. Martin	Houston	#13
J.D. Hudson	VA	#14
J. F. Nolan	WI	#15

Thanks to those of you who have contributed stories for this issue. Submitted stories not appearing will be included in the next newsletter.

If your regional column, in comparison to the others, doesn't quite measure up (especially in the area of sales success stories) now is the time to take action and develop the Rep Rap habit.

Send your story to your Regional Manager. He is responsible for gathering and embellishing this information and directing it to the Rep Rap editor.

REP/RAP

Product Showcase

HOSTILE*LITE*®

EM & EB Series

EXPLOSION-PROOF, DUST IGNITION-PROOF FIXTURES IN A COMPACT, COST-SAVING SIZE

With the addition of the EM and EB Series, Killark's hazardous location lighting package now ranks among the industry's finest.

Like their mogul base (EZ Series) counterpart, these rugged and compact luminaires have been engineered to meet and exceed the most rigorous application requirements of industrial users and electrical specifiers and contractors.

EM and EB Series fixtures accommodate five different light sources, including medium base incandescent and HID lamps, plus PL fluorescent lamps. Your customers

will appreciate this flexibility as well as realizing long-term benefits of corrosion-resistant construction and cost-saving design features.

All of this and more is conveyed in the new 12-page, 4-color EM & EB Series sales brochure. Your personal copy is enclosed, along with a companion 16-page booklet of photometrics and other supporting information.

The opportunity has never been greater, says Lighting Product Manager Gary Davis, to generate specifications and write orders for Killark lighting products.

Check out this list of great features

Medium Base Incandescent EMI SERIES	Bi-Pin Base Fluorescent EBF SERIES	Medium Base HPS, MH & MV EMS, EMH, EMM SERIES
Lowest initial cost	Long lamp life	Greatest energy savings
— QUALITY FEATURES —	— QUALITY FEATURES —	— QUALITY FEATURES —
• Three fixture configurations accommodate lamps through 300 watts	• Accommodates one or two 13 watts PL twin tube lamps	• HPS 35 through 150 watt MH 50, 70, 100 watt MV 50, 75, 100 watt
• Glazed white porcelain socket rated 660W-600V	• GX23 Bi-Pin base thermoplastic socket	• Glazed white porcelain socket pulse rated 4KV
• UL-844 listed	• UL-844 listed	• UL-844 listed
• UL-595 (marine)	• UL-595 (marine)	• UL-595 (marine)
• NEMA 4X rated	• NEMA 4X rated	• NEMA 4X rated
• Corrosion-resistant construction	• Corrosion-resistant construction	• Corrosion-resistant construction
• Wireless assembly of ballast tank to mounting cap	• Wireless assembly of ballast tank to mounting cap	• Wireless assembly of ballast tank to mounting cap

NEW DBF SERIES FLUORESCENT

Sent out as Killark's Weekly Mailing of October 23, you should have in your possession a DBF Series information package.

As you will discover, this new offering will allow you to effectively participate in the 6 million dollar market for Class I, Division 2 and Class II, Division 2 fluorescent fixtures.

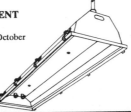

Get CONNECTED

PROMOTION RESULTS

Fittings Product Manager Brad Dearborn reports a successful conclusion to our 1992 Connector promotion. Brad says we surpassed 1991 sales (for the same period) by an impressive amount.

We extend our congratulations to the following Killark representatives who have met or exceeded their goals.

	Ranking by Performance
Steve Lytle	#1
Lesco	#2
Fox, Rowden, McBrayer	#3
Agents West	#4
Bill Collin	#5
Warshaw	#6
Brett Polk	#7
Tom Gorin	#8
J.D. Martin	#9
Electrical Agencies	#10
Joe Bertsch	#11
Rich Diego	#12
J. F. Nolan	#13
David Rak	#14
J.D. Martin	#15
Buchanan/Fields	#16
J.D. Hudson	#17
Electra Sales	#18
Bu-Nell	#19
Goldberg/McGrinder	#20
Curtis Stout	#21

Your comments and feedback were most helpful in this promotion. Similar performance-based programs for 1993 are now on the drawing board.

Shown above (left) is Dave Azbill (Aztex Eng. Co., Houston, TX) presenting Killark Specification Engineer Frank Hogan with the R.W. Mills Award. This is the most prestigious award the IEE Petroleum Chemical Industry Committee can bestow on a member. Frank serves as PCIC's Publicity Chairman and is an active member of the Executive Sub-Committee.

4

HUBBELL KILLARK®

Index

About the Author

Steve Levit is principal of SLA, a consultancy firm that has assisted many companies in adopting such world-class operating methods as TQM, JIT, EDI, and others. He is an expert in implementing the full range of improvement strategies, including quality circles, CIM, high performance teams, and time-based competition.
Mr. Levit writes frequently on these topics, and also speaks at universities, professional organizations, public- and industry-sponsored seminars, and customized in-house training sessions.